"This report is, as you know, the first of its kind ever made by a President to the Congress .... It is, in my view, the most comprehensive statement on foreign and defense policy ever made in this country. . . .

"It also is historic because it, in effect, marks a watershed, a watershed in American foreign policy. . . . This report, as you will note from reading the introduction particularly and the various pages in it, shows a very significant shift from those policies of the past to the new policies dealing with the world situation as it is today.

• • •

"[It] also represents, speaking for myself, the experience that I have had, . . . going back over twenty-two years, and reflects my best view at this time of where we are and where we ought to go. . . .

• • •

"I commend the report to your reading."

—Remarks of the President
before delivery of the
Report to Congress,
February 16, 1970

UNITED STATES FOREIGN POLICY FOR THE 1970's:

A New Strategy for Peace

The President's report to the Congress and the nation on American foreign policy

A NATIONAL GENERAL COMPANY

No copyright is claimed in textual
materials of this volume which are a publication
of the United States government.

UNITED STATES FOREIGN POLICY FOR THE 1970'S:
A NEW STRATEGY FOR PEACE
A Bantam Book / published June 1970

Published simultaneously in the United States and Canada

Bantam Books are published by Bantam Books, Inc., a National General company. Its trade-mark, consisting of the words "Bantam Books" and the portrayal of a bantam, is registered in the United States Patent Office and in other countries. Marca Registrada. Bantam Books, Inc., 666 Fifth Avenue, New York, N.Y. 10019.

PRINTED IN THE UNITED STATES OF AMERICA

TABLE OF CONTENTS

Introduction   1

PART I
THE NATIONAL SECURITY
COUNCIL SYSTEM   13

PART II
PARTNERSHIP AND THE
NIXON DOCTRINE   19
    Europe   19
    The Western Hemisphere   30
    Asia and the Pacific   40
    Vietnam   47
    The Middle East   59
    Africa   65
    International Economic Policy   71
    The United Nations   81

PART III
AMERICA'S STRENGTH   85
    Shaping Our Military Posture   85
    The Process of Defense Planning   87
    Strategic Policy   91
    General Purpose Forces   98

PART IV
AN ERA OF NEGOTIATION — 101
- The Soviet Union — 104
- Eastern Europe — 105
- Communist China — 107
- Arms Control — 109
- Issues for the Future — 116

CONCLUSION
A NEW DEFINITION OF PEACE — 117

INTRODUCTION

> "A nation needs many qualities, but it needs faith and confidence above all. Skeptics do not build societies; the idealists are the builders. Only societies that believe in themselves can rise to their challenges. Let us not, then, pose a false choice between meeting our responsibilities abroad and meeting the needs of our people at home. We shall meet both or we shall meet neither."
>
> The President's Remarks
> at the Air Force Academy
> Commencement, June 4, 1969.

When I took office, the most immediate problem facing our nation was the war in Vietnam. No question has more occupied our thoughts and energies during this past year.

Yet the fundamental task confronting us was more profound. We could see that the whole pattern of international politics was changing. Our challenge was to understand that change, to define America's goals for the next period, and to set in motion policies to achieve them. For all Americans must understand that because of its strength, its history and its concern for human dignity, this nation occupies a special place in the world. Peace and progress are impossible without a major American role.

This first annual report on U.S. foreign policy is more than a record of one year. It is this Administration's statement of a new approach to foreign policy, to match a new era of international relations.

A New Era

The postwar period in international relations has ended.

Then, we were the only great power whose society and economy had escaped World War II's massive destruction. Today, the ravages of that war have been overcome. Western Europe and Japan have recovered their economic strength, their political vitality, and their national self-confidence. Once the recipients of American aid, they have now begun to share their growing resources with the developing world. Once almost totally dependent on American military power, our European allies now play a greater role in our common policies, commensurate with their growing strength.

Then, new nations were being born, often in turmoil and uncertainty. Today, these nations have a new spirit and a growing strength of independence. Once, many feared that they would become simply a battleground of cold-war rivalry and fertile ground for Communist penetration. But this fear misjudged their pride in their national identities and their determination to preserve their newly won sovereignty.

Then, we were confronted by a monolithic Communist world. Today, the nature of that world has changed—the power of individual Communist nations has grown, but international Communist unity has been shattered. Once a unified bloc, its solidarity has been broken by the powerful forces of nationalism. The Soviet Union and Communist China, once bound by an alliance of friendship, had become bitter adversaries by the mid-1960's. The only times the Soviet Union has used the Red Army since World War II have been against its own allies—in East Germany in 1953, in Hungary in 1956, and in Czechoslovakia in 1968. The Marxist dream of international Communist unity has disintegrated.

Then, the United States had a monopoly or overwhelming superiority of nuclear weapons. Today, a revolution in the technology of war has altered the nature of the military balance of power. New types of weapons present new dangers. Communist China has acquired thermonuclear weapons. Both the Soviet Union and the United States have acquired the ability to inflict unacceptable damage on the other, no matter which strikes first. There can be no gain and certainly no victory for the power that provokes a thermonuclear exchange. Thus, both sides have recognized a vital mutual interest in halting the dangerous momentum of the nuclear arms race.

Then, the slogans formed in the past century were the ideological accessories of the intellectual debate. Today, the "isms" have lost their vitality—indeed the restlessness of youth on both sides of the dividing line testifies to the need for a new idealism and deeper purposes.

This is the challenge and the opportunity before America as it enters the 1970's.

The Framework for a Durable Peace

In the first postwar decades, American energies were absorbed in coping with a cycle of recurrent crises, whose fundamental origins lay in the destruction of World War II and the tensions attending the emergence of scores of new nations. Our opportunity today—and challenge—is to get at the causes of crises, to take a longer view, and to help build the international relationships that will provide the framework of a durable peace.

I have often reflected on the meaning of "peace," and have reached one certain conclusion: Peace must be far more than the absence of war. Peace must provide a durable structure of international relationships which inhibits or removes the causes of war. Building a lasting peace requires a foreign policy guided by three basic principles:

—Peace requires *partnership*. Its obligations, like its benefits, must be shared. This concept of partnership guides our relations with all friendly nations.
—Peace requires *strength*. So long as there are those who would threaten our vital interests and those of our allies with military force, we must be strong. American weakness could tempt would-be aggressors to make dangerous miscalculations.
At the same time, our own strength is important only in relation to the strength of others. We—like others—must place high priority on enhancing our security through cooperative arms control.
—Peace requires a *willingness to negotiate*. All nations—and we are no exception—have important national interests to protect. But the most fundamental interest of all nations lies in building the structure of peace. In partnership with our allies, secure in our own strength, we will seek those areas in which we can agree among ourselves

and with others to accommodate conflicts and overcome rivalries. We are working toward the day when *all* nations will have a stake in peace, and will therefore be partners in its maintenance.

Within such a structure, international disputes can be settled and clashes contained. The insecurity of nations, out of which so much conflict arises, will be eased, and the habits of moderation and compromise will be nurtured. Most important, a durable peace will give full opportunity to the powerful forces driving toward economic change and social justice.

This vision of a peace built on partnership, strength and willingness to negotiate is the unifying theme of this report. In the sections that follow, the first steps we have taken during this past year—the policies we have devised and the programs we have initiated to realize this vision—are placed in the context of these three principles.

1. PEACE THROUGH PARTNERSHIP—THE NIXON DOCTRINE As I said in my address of November 3, "We Americans are a do-it-yourself people—an impatient people. Instead of teaching someone else to do a job, we like to do it ourselves. This trait has been carried over into our foreign policy."

The postwar era of American foreign policy began in this vein in 1947 with the proclamation of the Truman Doctrine and the Marshall Plan, offering American economic and military assistance to countries threatened by aggression. Our policy held that democracy and prosperity, buttressed by American military strength and organized in a worldwide network of American-led alliances, would insure stability and peace. In the formative years of the postwar period, this great effort of international political and economic reconstruction was a triumph of American leadership and imagination, especially in Europe.

For two decades after the end of the Second World War, our foreign policy was guided by such a vision and inspired by its success. The vision was based on the fact that the United States was the richest and most stable country, without whose initiative and resources little security or progress was possible.

This impulse carried us through into the 1960's. The United States conceived programs and ran them. We devised strategies, and proposed them to our allies. We discerned dangers, and acted directly to combat them.

The world has dramatically changed since the days of the Marshall Plan. We deal now with a world of stronger allies, a community of independent developing nations, and a Communist world still hostile but now divided.

Others now have the ability and responsibility to deal with local disputes which once might have required our intervention. Our contribution and success will depend not on the frequency of our involvement in the affairs of others, but on the stamina of our policies. This is the approach which will best encourage other nations to do their part, and will most genuinely enlist the support of the American people.

This is the message of the doctrine I announced at Guam—the "Nixon Doctrine." Its central thesis is that the United States will participate in the defense and development of allies and friends, but that America cannot—and will not—conceive *all* the plans, design *all* the programs, execute *all* the decisions and undertake *all* the defense of the free nations of the world. We will help where it makes a real difference and is considered in our interest.

America cannot live in isolation if it expects to live in peace. We have no intention of withdrawing from the world. The only issue before us is how we can be most effective in meeting our responsibilities, protecting our interests, and thereby building peace.

A more responsible participation by our foreign friends in their own defense and progress means a more effective common effort toward the goals we all seek. Peace in the world will continue to require us to maintain our commitments—and we will. As I said at the United Nations, "It is not my belief that the way to peace is by giving up our friends or letting down our allies." But a more balanced and realistic American role in the world is essential if American commitments are to be sustained over the long pull. In my State of the Union Address, I affirmed that "to insist that other nations play a role is not a retreat from responsibility; it is a sharing of responsibility." This is not a way for America to withdraw from its indispensable role in the world. It is a way—the only way—we can carry out our responsibilities.

It is misleading, moreover, to pose the fundamental question so largely in terms of commitments. Our objective, in the first instance, is to support our *interests* over the long run with a sound foreign policy. The more that policy is based on a realistic assessment of our and others' interests, the more effective our role in the world can be. We are not involved in the world because we have commitments; we have commitments because we are involved. Our interests must shape our commitments, rather than the other way around.

We will view new commitments in the light of a careful assessment of our own national interests and those of other countries, of the specific threats to those interests, and of our capacity to counter those threats at an acceptable risk and cost.

We have been guided by these concepts during the past year in our dealings with free nations throughout the world.

—In Europe, our policies embody precisely the three principles of a durable peace: partnership, continued strength to defend our common interests when challenged, and willingness to negotiate differences with adversaries.
—Here in the Western Hemisphere we seek to strengthen our special relationship with our sister republics through a new program of action for progress in which all voices are heard and none predominates.
—In Asia, where the Nixon Doctrine was enunciated, partnership will have special meaning for our policies—as evidenced by our strengthened ties with Japan. Our cooperation with Asian nations will be enhanced as they cooperate with another and develop regional institutions.
—In Vietnam, we seek a just settlement which all parties to the conflict, and all Americans, can support. We are working closely with the South Vietnamese to strengthen

their ability to defend themselves. As South Vietnam grows stronger, the other side will, we hope, soon realize that it becomes ever more in their interest to negotiate a just peace.

—In the Middle East, we shall continue to work with others to establish a possible framework within which the parties to the Arab-Israeli conflict can negotiate the complicated and difficult questions at issue. Others must join us in recognizing that a settlement will require sacrifices and restraints by all concerned.

—Africa, with its historic ties to so many of our own citizens, must always retain a significant place in our partnership with the new nations. Africans will play the major role in fulfilling their just aspirations—an end to racialism, the building of new nations, freedom from outside interference, and cooperative economic development. But we will add our efforts to theirs to help realize Africa's great potential.

—In an ever more interdependent world economy, American foreign policy will emphasize the freer flow of capital and goods between nations. We are proud to have participated in the successful cooperative effort which created Special Drawing Rights, a form of international money which will help insure the stability of the monetary structure on which the continued expansion of trade depends.

—The great effort of economic development must engage the cooperation of all nations. We are carefully studying the specific goals of our economic assistance programs and how most effectively to reach them.

—Unprecedented scientific and technological advances as well as explosions in population, communications, and knowledge require new forms of international cooperation. The United Nations, the symbol of international partnership, will receive our continued strong support as it marks its 25th Anniversary.

2. AMERICA'S STRENGTH The second element of a durable peace must be America's strength. Peace, we have learned, cannot be gained by good will alone.

In determining the strength of our defenses, we must make precise and crucial judgments. We should spend no more than is necessary. But there is an irreducible minimum of essential military security: for if we are less strong than necessary, and if the worst happens, there will be no domestic society to look after. The magnitude of such a catastrophe, and the reality of the opposing military power that could threaten it, present a risk which requires of any President the most searching and careful attention to the state of our defenses.

The changes in the world since 1945 have altered the context and requirements of our defense policy. In this area, perhaps more than in any other, the need to re-examine our approaches is urgent and constant.

The last 25 years have seen a revolution in the nature of military power. In fact, there has been a series of transformations—from the atomic to the thermonuclear weapon, from the strategic bomber to the intercontinental ballistic missile, from the surface missile to the hardened silo and the missile-carrying submarine, from the single to the multiple warhead, and from air defense to missile defense. We are now entering an era in which the sophistication and destructiveness of weapons present more formidable and complex issues affecting our strategic posture.

The last 25 years have also seen an important change in the relative balance of strategic power. From 1945 to 1949, we were the only nation in the world possessing an arsenal of atomic weapons. From 1950 to 1966, we possessed an overwhelming superiority in strategic weapons. From 1967 to 1969, we retained a significant superiority. Today, the Soviet Union possesses a powerful and sophisticated strategic force approaching our own. We must consider, too, that Communist China will deploy its own intercontinental missiles during the coming decade, introducing new and complicating factors for our strategic planning and diplomacy.

In the light of these fateful changes, the Administration undertook a comprehensive and far-reaching reconsideration of the premises and procedures for designing our forces. We sought—and I believe we have achieved—a rational and coherent formulation of our defense strategy and requirements for the 1970's.

The importance of comprehensive planning of policy and objective scrutiny of programs is clear:

—Because of the lead-time in building new strategic systems, the decisions we make today substantially determine our military posture—and thus our security—five years from now. This places a premium on foresight and planning.
—Because the allocation of national resources between defense programs and other national programs is itself an issue of policy, it must be considered on a systematic basis at the early stages of the national security planning process.
—Because we are a leader of the Atlantic Alliance, our doctrine and forces are crucial to the policy and planning of NATO. The mutual confidence that holds the allies together depends on understanding, agreement, and coordination among the 15 sovereign nations of the Treaty.
—Because our security depends not only on our own strategic strength, but also on cooperative efforts to provide greater security for everyone through arms control, planning weapons systems and planning for arms control negotiations must be closely integrated.

For these reasons, this Administration has established procedures for the intensive scrutiny of defense issues in the light of overall national priorities. We have re-examined our strategic forces; we have reassessed our general purpose forces; and we have engaged in the most painstaking preparation ever undertaken by the United States Government for arms control negotiations.

3. WILLINGNESS TO NEGOTIATE—AN ERA OF NEGOTIATION Partnership and strength are two of the pillars of the structure of a durable peace. Negotiation is the third. For our commitment to peace is most convincingly demonstrated in our willingness to negotiate our points of difference in a fair and businesslike manner with the Communist countries.

We are under no illusions. We know that there are enduring ideological differences. We are aware of the difficulty in moderating tensions that arise from the clash of national interests. These differences will not be dissipated by changes of atmosphere or dissolved in cordial personal relations between statesmen. They involve strong convictions and contrary philosophies, necessities of national security, and the deep-seated differences of perspectives formed by geography and history.

The United States, like any other nation, has interests of its own, and will defend those interests. But any nation today must define its interests with special concern for the interests of others. If some nations define their security in a manner that means insecurity for other nations, then peace is threatened and the security of all is diminished. This obligation is particularly great for the nuclear superpowers on whose decisions the survival of mankind may well depend.

The United States is confident that tensions can be eased and the danger of war reduced by patient and precise efforts to reconcile conflicting interests on concrete issues. Coexistence demands more than a spirit of good will. It requires the definition of positive goals which can be sought and achieved cooperatively. It requires real progress toward resolution of specific differences. This is our objective.

As the Secretary of State said on December 6:

"We will continue to probe every available opening that offers a prospect for better East-West relations, for the resolution of problems large or small, for greater security for all. In this the United States will continue to play an active role in concert with our allies."

This is the spirit in which the United States ratified the Non-Proliferation Treaty and entered into negotiation with the Soviet Union on control of the military use of the seabeds, on the framework of a settlement in the Middle East, and on limitation of strategic arms. This is the basis on which we and our Atlantic allies have offered to negotiate on concrete issues affecting the security and future of Europe, and on which the United States took steps last year to improve our relations with nations of Eastern Europe. This is also the spirit in which we have resumed formal talks in Warsaw with Communist China. No nation need be our permanent enemy.

America's Purpose

These policies were conceived as a result of change, and we know they will be tested by the change that lies ahead. The world of 1970 was not predicted a decade ago, and we can be certain that the world of 1980 will render many current views obsolete.

The source of America's historic greatness has been our ability to see what had to be done, and then to do it. I believe America now has the chance to move the world closer to a durable peace. And I know that Americans working with each other and with other nations can make our vision real.

PART I

THE NATIONAL SECURITY COUNCIL SYSTEM

If we were to establish a new foreign policy for the era to come, we had to begin with a basic restructuring of the process by which policy is made.

Our fresh purposes demanded new methods of planning and a more rigorous and systematic process of policymaking. We required a system which would summon and gather the best ideas, the best analyses and the best information available to the government and the nation.

Efficient procedure does not insure wisdom in the substance of policy. But given the complexity of contemporary choices, adequate procedures are an indispensable component of the act of judgment. I have long believed that the most pressing issues are not necessarily the most fundamental ones; we know that an effective American policy requires clarity of purpose for the future as well as a procedure for dealing with the present. We do not want to exhaust ourselves managing crises; our basic goal is to shape the future.

At the outset, therefore, I directed that the National Security Council be reestablished as the principal forum for Presidential consideration of foreign policy issues. The revitalized Council—composed by statute of the President, the Vice President, the Secretaries of State and Defense, and the Director of the Office of Emergency Preparedness—and its new system of supporting groups are designed to respond to the requirements of leadership in the 1970's:

—Our policy must be *creative*: foreign policy must mean more than reacting to emergencies; we must fashion a new and positive vision of a peaceful world, and design new policies to achieve it.

—Our policymaking must be *systematic*: our actions must be the products of thorough analysis, forward planning, and deliberate decision. We must master problems before they master us.

—We must know the *facts*: intelligent discussions in the National Security Council and wise decisions require the most reliable information available. Disputes in the government have been caused too often by an incomplete awareness or understanding of the facts.

—We must know the *alternatives*: we must know what our real options are and not simply what compromise has found bureaucratic acceptance. Every view and every alternative must have a fair hearing. Presidential leadership is not the same as ratifying bureaucratic consensus.

—We must be prepared if *crises* occur: we must anticipate crises where possible. If they cannot be prevented, we must plan for dealing with them. All the elements of emergency action, political as well as military, must be related to each other.

—Finally, we must have effective *implementation*: it does little good to plan intelligently and imaginatively if our decisions are not well carried out.

Creativity: Above all, a foreign policy for the 1970's demands imaginative thought. In a world of onrushing change, we can no longer rest content with familiar ideas or assume that the future will be a projection of the present. If we are to meet both the peril and the opportunity of change, we require a clear and positive vision of the world we seek—and of America's contribution to bringing it about.

As modern bureaucracy has grown, the understanding of change and the formulation of new purposes have become more difficult. Like men, governments find old ways hard to change and new paths difficult to discover.

The mandate I have given to the National Security Council system, and the overriding objective of every policy review undertaken, is to clarify our view of where we want to be in the next three to five years. Only then can we ask, and answer, the question of how to proceed.

In central areas of policy, we have arranged our procedure of policymaking so as to address the broader questions of long-term objectives first; we define our purposes, and then address the specific operational issues. In this manner, for example, the NSC first addressed the basic questions of the rationale and doctrine of our strategic posture, and then considered—in the light of new criteria of strategic sufficiency—our specific weapons programs and our specific policy for the negotiations on strategic arms limitation. We determined that our relationship with Japan for the 1970's and beyond had to be founded on our mutual and increasingly collaborative concern for peace and security in the Far East; we then addressed the issue of Okinawa's status in the light of this fundamental objective.

Systematic Planning: American foreign policy must not be merely the result of a series of piecemeal tactical decisions forced by the pressures of events. If our policy is to embody a coherent vision of the world and a rational conception of America's interests, our specific actions must be the products of rational and deliberate choice. We need a system which forces consideration of problems before they become emergencies, which enables us to make our basic determinations of purpose before being pressed by events, and to mesh policies.

The National Security Council itself met 37 times in 1969, and considered over a score of different major problems of national security. Each Council meeting was the culmination of an interagency process of systematic and comprehensive review.

This is how the process works: I assign an issue to an Interdepartmental Group—chaired by an Assistant Secretary of State—for intensive study, asking it to formulate the policy choices and to analyze the pros and cons of the different courses of action. This group's report is examined by an interagency Review Group of senior officials—chaired by the Assistant to the President for National Security Affairs—to insure that the issues, options, and views are presented fully and fairly. The paper is then presented to me and the full National Security Council.

Some topics requiring specialized knowledge are handled through different channels before reaching the National Security Council. But the purpose is the same—systematic review and analysis, bringing together all the agencies concerned:

—The major issues of defense policy are treated in systematic and integrated fashion by the NSC Defense Program Review Committee. This group reviews at the Under Secretary level the major defense policy and program issues which have strategic, political, diplomatic, and economic implications in relation to overall national priorities.

—Through other NSC interagency groups, the United States Government has undertaken its first substantial effort to review all its resource programs within certain countries on a systematic and integrated basis, instead of haphazardly and piecemeal.

Determination of the Facts: Intelligent discussions and decisions at the highest level demand the fullest possible information. Too often in the past, the process of policy-making has been impaired or distorted by incomplete information, and by disputes in the government which resulted from the lack of a common appreciation of the facts. It is an essential function of the NSC system, therefore, to bring together all the agencies of the government concerned with foreign affairs to elicit, assess, and present to me and the Council all the pertinent knowledge available.

Normally NSC Interdepartmental Groups are assigned this task. But other interagency groups perform this function for certain special topics. For example:

—The Verification Panel was formed to gather the essential facts relating to a number of important issues of strategic arms limitation, such as Soviet strategic capabilities, and our potential means of verifying compliance with various possible agreements. This panel was designed not to induce agreement on policy views, but to establish as firmly as possible the *data* on which to base policy discussions. It helped to resolve many major policy differences which might otherwise have been intractable. As the section on Arms Control in this report explains in detail, the Panel played a central part in making our preparation for the Strategic Arms Limitation Talks with the Soviet Union the most thorough in which the U.S. Government has ever engaged.

—The Vietnam Special Studies Group (VSSG) gathers and presents to the highest levels of the United States Government the fullest and most up-to-date information on trends and conditions in the countryside in Vietnam. This group is of key assistance in our major and sustained effort to understand the factors which will determine the course of Vietnamization.

Full Range of Options: I do not believe that Presidential leadership consists merely in ratifying a consensus reached among departments and agencies. The President bears the Constitutional responsibility of making the judgments and decisions that form our policy.

The new NSC system is designed to make certain that clear policy choices reach the top, so that the various positions can be fully debated in the meeting of the Council. Differences of view are identified and defended, rather than muted or buried. I refuse to be confronted with a bureaucratic consensus that leaves me no options but acceptance or rejection, and that gives me no way of knowing what alternatives exist.

The NSC system also insures that all agencies and departments receive a fair hearing before I make my decisions. All Departments concerned with a problem participate on the groups that draft and review the policy papers. They know that their positions and arguments will reach the Council without dilution, along with the other alternatives. Council meetings are not rubber-stamp sessions. And as my decisions are reached they are circulated in writing, so that all departments concerned are fully informed of our policy, and so that implementation can be monitored.

Crisis Planning: Some events in the world over which we have little control may produce crises that we cannot prevent, even though our systematized study forewarns us of their possibility. But we can be the masters of events when crises occur, to the extent that we are able to prepare ourselves in advance.

For this purpose, we created within the NSC system a special senior panel known as the Washington Special Actions Group (WSAG). This group drafts contingency plans for possible crises, integrating the political and military requirements of crisis action. The action responsibilities of the departments of the Government are planned in detail, and specific responsibilities assigned in an agreed time sequence in advance. While no one can anticipate exactly the timing and course of a possible crisis, the WSAG's planning helps insure that we have asked the right questions in advance, and thought through the implications of various responses.

Policy Implementation: The variety and complexity of foreign policy issues in today's world places an enormous premium on the effective implementation of policy. Just as our policies are shaped and our programs formed through a constant process of interagency discussion and debate within the NSC framework, so the implementation of our major policies needs review and coordination on a continuing basis. This is done by an interdepartmental committee at the Under Secretary level chaired by the Under Secretary of State.

Conclusions

There is no textbook prescription for organizing the machinery of policymaking, and no procedural formula for making wise decisions. The policies of this Administration will be judged on their results, not on how methodically they were made.

The NSC system is meant to help us address the fundamental issues, clarify our basic purposes, examine all alternatives, and plan intelligent actions. It is meant to promote the thoroughness and deliberation which are essential for an effective American foreign policy. It gives us the means to bring to bear the best foresight and insight of which the nation is capable.

PART II

PARTNERSHIP AND THE NIXON DOCTRINE

Europe

> "I believe we must build an alliance strong enough to deter those who would threaten war; close enough to provide for continuous and far-reaching consultation; trusting enough to accept a diversity of views; realistic enough to deal with the world as it is; flexible enough to explore new channels of constructive cooperation."
>
> Address by the President
> to the North Atlantic
> Council, April 10, 1969

The peace of Europe is crucial to the peace of the world. This truth, a lesson learned at a terrible cost twice in the Twentieth Century, is a central principle of United States foreign policy. For the foreseeable future, Europe must be the cornerstone of the structure of a durable peace.

Since 1945, the nations of Western Europe and North America have built together an alliance and a mutual respect worthy of the values and heritage we share. Our partnership is founded not merely on a common perception of common dangers but on a shared vision of a better world.

It was essential, therefore, that my first trip abroad as President should be to the capitals of our Western European allies. It was time to reaffirm the importance of those ties, and to strengthen the collaboration with which we shall develop, together, new policies for the new issues of the 1970's.

We must adapt to the conditions created by the past successes of our alliance. European politics are more fluid, and the issues facing the alliance are more subtle and profound, than ever in the past 20 years. These issues challenge our mastery of each of the three elements of a durable peace:

—Genuine *partnership* must increasingly characterize our alliance. For if we cannot maintain and develop further such a relationship with our North Atlantic allies, the prospects for achieving it with our other friends and allies around the world are slim indeed. But the evolution—past and future—of Europe and of European-American relations presents new issues. We must change the pattern of American predominance, appropriate to the postwar era, to match the new circumstances of today. We must extend our joint endeavor into another dimension of common challenges—bringing Twentieth Century man and his environment to terms with one another in modern industrial societies.

—Jointly with our allies we must maintain the *strength* required to defend our common interests against external dangers, so long as those dangers exist. We have learned to integrate our forces; we now need better means of harmonizing our policies. We need a rational alliance defense posture for the longer term. This requires a common understanding of the nature of the dangers today and tomorrow, and on nuclear and non-nuclear strategy and forces. We must fashion common policies for the pursuit of security through arms control, as well as through military strength.

—Together with our allies, we must be prepared to *negotiate*. The problems and dangers of the division of Europe persist. Our association with our friends and allies in Europe is the starting point from which we seek to resolve those problems and cope with those dangers. Our efforts to pursue genuine relaxation of tensions between East and West will be a test of the new trans-Atlantic partnership.

A New and Mature Partnership

I went to Western Europe in February 1969 to reaffirm America's commitment to partnership with Europe.

A reaffirmation was sorely needed. We had to re-establish the principle and practice of consultation. For too long in the past, the United States had led without listening, talked to our allies instead of *with* them, and informed them of new departures instead of deciding with them. Inspired by the success of the Marshall Plan, we had taken such pride in our leadership of the alliance that we forgot how much even the origin and success of the Marshall Plan grew from European ideas and European efforts as well as our own.

After 20 years, the economic prostration, military weakness, and political instability in postwar Europe that had required a predominant American effort were things of the past. Our *common* success in rebuilding Western Europe had restored our allies to their proper strength and status. It was time that our own leadership, in its substance and its manner, took account of this fact. As I stated to the NATO Council in Brussels on my trip in February 1969:

"The nations of NATO are rich in physical resources—but they are even richer in their accumulated wisdom and their experience of the world today. In fashioning America's policies, we need the benefit of that wisdom and that experience."

But the issue we face is not simply improved communication. It is the fundamental question of what shall be the content and purpose of the European-American relationship in the 1970's. In today's world, what kind of an alliance shall we strive to build?

Last April, the North Atlantic Treaty completed its second decade and began its third. I stated on that occasion:

"When NATO was founded, the mere fact of cooperation among the Western nations was of tremendous significance, both symbolically and substantively. Now the symbol is not enough; we need substance. The alliance today will be judged by the content of its cooperation, not merely by its form."

The durability of the alliance itself is a triumph, but also a challenge: It would be unreasonable to imagine that a structure and relationship developed in the late 1940's can remain the same in content and purpose in the 1970's.

The fundamentals of the relationship are not in question. The original aims of the Western Alliance are still our basic purposes: the defense of Western Europe against common challenges, and ultimately the creation of a viable and secure European order.

But what pattern of relations will serve these objectives best today? There is a natural tendency to prefer the status quo and to support established forms and relationships that have served well in the past. But we can see in 1970 that there is no "status quo"—the only constant is the inevitability of change. Evolution within Western Europe has changed the region's position in the world, and therefore its role in the Western Alliance.

Since 1945, West Germany achieved a position of mutual respect and partnership with its Western neighbors. From this reconciliation a larger European entity has developed, with prospects of further growth. Americans have welcomed this transformation and see it as a vindication of the historic choices made twenty years ago. We contributed, not only by insuring the physical safety of Western Europe from outside attack or pressure, and in the early years by providing economic support, but also by giving a powerful impetus to the building of European institutions.

But today, European vitality is more self-sustaining. The preponderant American influence that was a natural consequence of postwar conditions would be self-defeating today. For nations which did not share in the responsibility to make the vital decisions for their own defense and diplomacy could retain neither their self-respect nor their self-assurance.

A more balanced association and a more genuine partnership are in America's interest. As this progress advances, the balance of burdens and responsibilities must gradually be adjusted, to reflect the economic and political realities of European progress. Our allies will deserve a voice in the alliance and its decisions commensurate with their growing power and contributions.

As we move from dominance to partnership, there is the possibility that some will see this as a step towards disengagement. But in the third decade of our commitment to Europe, the depth of our relationship is a fact of life. We can no more disengage from Europe than from Alaska.

We recognize that America's contribution will continue to be unique in certain areas, such as in maintaining a nuclear deterrent and a level of involvement sufficient to balance the powerful military position of the USSR in Eastern Europe. But we have no desire to occupy such a position in Europe that European affairs are not the province of the sovereign states that conduct them.

Intra-European institutions are in flux. We favor a definition by Western Europe of a distinct identity, for the sake of its own continued vitality and independence of spirit. Our support for the strengthening and broadening of the European Community has not diminished. We recognize that our interests will necessarily be affected by Europe's evolution, and we may have to make sacrifices in the common interest. We consider that the possible economic price of a truly unified Europe is outweighed by the gain in the political vitality of the West as a whole.

The structure of Western Europe itself—the organization of its unity—is fundamentally the concern of the Europeans. We cannot unify Europe and we do not believe that there is only one road to that goal. When the United States in previous Administrations turned into an ardent advocate, it harmed rather than helped progress.

We believe that we can render support to the process of European coalescence not only by our role in the North Atlantic Alliance and by our relationships with European institutions, but also by our bilateral relations with the several European countries. For many years to come, these relations will provide essential trans-Atlantic bonds; and we will therefore continue to broaden and deepen them.

European Defense and Security

In choosing a strategy for our general purpose forces for the 1970's, we decided to continue our support for the present NATO strategy. And the Secretary of State and the Secretary of Defense announced at the NATO Council meeting in December that we would maintain current U.S. troop levels in Europe at least through mid-1971.

At the same time, we recognized that we must use this time to conduct a thorough study of our strategy for the defense of Western Europe, including a full and candid exchange of views with our allies.

The need for this study is based on several considerations:

First, at the beginning of the last decade the United States possessed overwhelming nuclear superiority over the Soviet Union. However, that superiority has been reduced by the growth in Soviet strategic forces during the 1960's. As I point out elsewhere, the prospect for the 1970's is that the Soviets will possess strategic forces approaching and in some categories exceeding our own.

This fundamental change in the strategic balance raises important questions about the relative role of strategic nuclear forces, conventional forces, and tactical nuclear weapons.

Second, there are several views among Western strategists concerning the answers to several key questions:

—What is a realistic assessment of the military threats to Western Europe that should be used as the basis for Allied strategic and force structure planning?
—For how long could NATO sustain a conventional forward defense against a determined Warsaw Pact attack?
—Beyond their value as a deterrent to war, how should our tactical nuclear weapons in Europe be used to counter specific Warsaw Pact military threats?
—How does the contemplated use of tactical nuclear weapons affect the size, equipment and deployment of Allied conventional forces?

Third, even though the NATO Allies have reached agreement on the strategy of flexible response, there are disagreements about the burdens that should be borne by the several partners in providing the forces and other resources required by that strategy. Further, questions have been raised concerning whether, for example, our logistics support, the disposition of our forces in Europe, and our airlift and sealift capabilities are sufficient to meet the needs of the existing strategy.

These questions must be addressed in full consultation with our allies. This is the process we have followed in the preparations for and conduct of the strategic arms limitation talks with the Soviet Union. We are consulting our allies closely at every stage, not on a take-it-or-leave-it basis but by seeking their advice on the whole range of options we have under consideration.

In assessing our common security, we must not be satisfied with formal agreements which paper over dissimilar views on fundamental issues or with language that is acceptable precisely because it permits widely divergent interpretations. Disagreements must be faced openly and their bases carefully explored. Because our security is inseparable, we can afford the most candid exchange of views.

In the past year, in the NATO Nuclear Planning Group, where the Secretary of Defense represents this government, the allies have taken significant steps to explore the principal problems of defining a common political rationale for the resort to tactical nuclear weapons. The completion of this process in close collaboration with all of our allies, including those possessing national nuclear capabilities, will be a major contribution to the credible defense of Europe.

The forging of a common understanding on basic security issues will materially improve our ability to deal sensibly and realistically with the opportunities and pressures for change that we face, including suggestions in this country for substantial reductions of U.S. troop levels in Europe and the possibility that balanced force reductions could become a subject of East-West discussions.

An Era of Negotiation in Europe

Our association with Western Europe is fundamental to the resolution of the problems caused by the unnatural division of the continent. We recognize that the reunion of Europe will come about not from one spectacular negotiation, but from an extended historical process.

We must be under no illusion about the difficulties. As I remarked last April, addressing the NATO Council in Washington:

> "It is not enough to talk of relaxing tension, unless we keep in mind the fact that 20 years of tension were not caused by superficial misunderstandings. A change of mood is useful only if it reflects some change of mind about political purpose.
>
> "It is not enough to talk of European security in the abstract. We must know the elements of insecurity and how to remove them. Conferences are useful if they deal with concrete issues, which means they must, of course, be carefully prepared."

The division of Europe gives rise to a number of interrelated issues—the division of Germany, access to Berlin, the level of military forces on both sides of the line, the barriers to economic and cultural relations, and other issues. We are prepared to negotiate on these issues, in any suitable forum.

We have already joined with the three allies involved—the United Kingdom, France and the Federal Republic of Germany—in suggesting to the Soviet Union that an attempt should be made to improve the situation regarding Berlin. Even if progress on broader issues cannot soon be made, the elimination of recurrent crises around Berlin would be desirable.

Our German ally has also undertaken steps to seek a normalization of its relations with its Eastern neighbors. Since the problem of Germany remains the key to East-West problems in Europe, we would welcome such a normalization. Just as the postwar era has ended in

Western Europe, it is our hope that a more satisfactory and enduring order will come into being in the center of the continent.

Within NATO, meanwhile, we have joined with our allies in canvassing other issues that might offer prospects for fruitful negotiation, including the possibility of reciprocal adjustments in the military forces on both sides of the present demarcation line in Europe.

There is no dearth of subjects to negotiate. But there is no one way to go about it or any preferable forum. Relations between East and West must be dealt with on several levels and it would be wrong to believe that one single grand conference can encompass all existing relationships.

High on the agenda of the Western Alliance is the complex responsibility of integrating our individual and collective efforts. Together with our allies we shall seek to answer these questions: Should we consider the relaxation of tensions in terms of an overall settlement between NATO and the Warsaw Pact? Or is there scope for a series of bilateral efforts? What are the limits of bilateral efforts and how can they be related to the NATO system of consultations? What would be the contribution of a unified Western Europe?

Last April 10, in my talk at the Twentieth Anniversary Celebration of NATO, I stated this problem as follows:

> "Up to now, our discussions [within NATO] have mainly had to do with tactics—ways and means of carrying out the provisions of a treaty drawn a generation ago. We have discussed clauses in proposed treaties; in the negotiations to come, we must go beyond these to the processes which these future treaties will set in motion. We must shake off our preoccupation with formal structure to bring into focus a common world view."

Without such a general understanding on the issues and our respective roles, we run a risk of failures and frustrations which have nothing to do with the intentions of the principals, but which could result from starting a sequence of events that gets out of control.

In the last analysis, progress does not depend on us and our allies alone. The prospects for durable agreement also involve the attitudes, interests, and policies of the Soviet Union and their allies in Eastern Europe. Ultimately, a workable system of security embracing all of Europe will require a willingness on the part of the Soviet Union to normalize its own relations with Eastern Europe—to recover from its anachronistic fear of Germany, and to recognize that its own security and the stability of Central Europe can best be served by a structure of reconciliation. Only then will an era of negotiation in Europe culminate in an era of peace.

A New Dimension

The common concerns and purposes of the Western allies reach beyond the military and political dimensions of traditional alliances.

Article 2 of the North Atlantic Treaty anticipated these further dimensions of partnership by pledging the allies to "strengthening their free institutions, . . . promoting conditions of stability and well-being," and "encourag[ing] economic collaboration." These are not goals limited to the Treaty area. They go beyond partnership among allies, military security, and negotiations with adversaries. As I said last April, on NATO's twentieth anniversary, the relationship of Europe and the United States "also needs a social dimension to deal with our concern for the quality of life in this last third of the Twentieth Century."

At America's initiative, the alliance created in 1969 a Committee on the Challenges of Modern Society—to pool our skills, our intellects, and our inventiveness in finding new ways to use technology to enhance our environments, and not to destroy them. For as I said last April:

"The Western nations share common ideals and a common heritage. We are all advanced societies, sharing the benefits and the gathering torments of a rapidly advanced industrial technology. The industrial nations share no challenge more urgent than that of bringing 20th century man and his environment to terms with one another—of making the world fit for man and helping man to learn how to remain in harmony with the rapidly changing world."

If this view was not at first uniformly held among the Allied nations, it emerged with increasing strength as the matter was considered—evidence both of the validity of the proposition, and of the lessons learned and skills acquired in the course of two decades of intensive and detailed consultation and cooperation.

Environmental problems are secondary effects of technological change; international environmental cooperation is therefore an essential requirement of our age. This has now begun in the Committee on the Challenges of Modern Society. We have established a procedure whereby individual nations offer to "pilot" studies in a specific area and are responsible for making recommendations for action. Eight projects have been agreed upon. These are road safety, disaster relief, air pollution, sea pollution, inland water pollution, scientific knowledge and governmental decision-making, group and individual motivation, and regional planning. The United States is pilot nation for the first three of these.

A provision of the charter of the Committee on the Challenges of Modern Society looks to expanding the number of nations involved in these efforts, and to the support of similar undertakings in other international organizations such as the Organization for Economic Cooperation and Development, the Economic Commission for Europe, and the United Nations, which is holding a worldwide conference on environmental problems in 1972. We see this new dimension of international cooperation as an urgent and positive area of work. Cooperative research, technological exchange, education, institution building, and international regulatory agreements are all required to reverse the trend toward pollution of our planet's environment within this critical decade.

Agenda for the Future

The agenda for the future of American relations with Europe is implicit in the statement of the issues we face together:

—The evolution of a mature partnership reflecting the vitality and the independence of Western European nations;
—the continuation of genuine consultation with our allies on the nature of the threats to alliance security, on maintenance of a common and credible strategy, and on an appropriate and sustainable level of forces;
—the continuation of genuine consultations with our allies on the mutual interests affected by the U.S.-Soviet talks on strategic arms limitation;
—the development of a European-American understanding on our common purposes and respective roles in seeking a peaceful and stable order in all of Europe;
—the expansion of allied and worldwide cooperation in facing the common social and human challenges of modern societies.

In 1969, the United States and its allies discussed most of these issues—some in the context of new proposals, but most of them in the form of new questions. These questions will not be answered in a year. As I said last February in Brussels, "They deal with the vast sweep of history, they need the most thorough deliberations." The deliberations will continue; we have the chance today to build a tomorrow worthy of our common heritage.

The Western Hemisphere

"Understandably, perhaps, a feeling has arisen in many Latin American quarters that the United States 'no longer cares.'

"My answer to that is simple.

"We do care. I care. I have visited most of your countries. I have met most of your leaders. I have talked with your people. I have seen your great needs, as well as your great achievements.

"And I know this, in my heart as well as in my mind: if peace and freedom are to endure in the world, there is no task more urgent than lifting up the hungry and the helpless, and putting flesh on the dreams of those who yearn for a better life."

The President's remarks at the

Annual Meeting of the Inter-American Press Association, Washington, October 31, 1969

The Setting

This concern which I expressed last year is central to our policies in the Western Hemisphere. Our relationship with our sister republics has special relevance for this Administration's general approach to foreign relations. We must be able to forge a constructive relationship with nations historically linked to us if we are to do so with nations more removed.

A new spirit and a new approach were needed to pursue this objective in the Americas. It meant recalling our special relationship but changing our attitude to accommodate the forces of change. And it meant translating our new attitude into an action program for progress that offers cooperative action rather than paternal promises and panaceas.

Throughout our history we have accorded the other American nations a special place in our foreign policy. This unique relationship is rooted in geography, in a common Western heritage and in a shared historical experience of independence born through revolution.

This relationship has evolved over time. Our long and close political and economic association, and our articulation of the concept of hemispheric community, have been self-fulfilling: It is now a political and psychological fact that the relations between the United States and Latin America have a special meaning for us both. We share a concept of hemispheric community, as well as a web of treaties, commitments and organizations that deserves the name of an Inter-American System.

But the character of that relationship has not been immune to the upheavals and transformations of past decades. Indeed, the continuing challenge throughout this hemisphere's history has been how to redefine and readjust this special relationship to meet changed circumstances, new settings, different problems.

That challenge is all the more compelling today.

Forces of Change

The powerful tides of change that have transformed the world since the Second World War have also swept through the Western Hemisphere, particularly in the 1960's. They have altered the nature of our relationship, and the expectations and obligations that flow from it.

When this Administration took office, it was evident that United States policies and programs had not kept pace with these fundamental changes. The state of the hemisphere and of our relationship was satisfying neither to North nor South Americans:

—Our power overshadowed the formal relationship of equality and even our restrained use of this power was not wholly reassuring. As a result, tension between us grew.
—Too many of our development programs were made *for* our neighbors instead of *with* them. This directive and tutorial style clashed with the growing self-assertiveness and nationalism of the other Western Hemisphere nations.
—Development problems had become more intense and complex; exploding population growth and accelerating urbanization added to social stress; frustrations were rising as expectations outstripped accomplishments.
—Political and social instability were therefore on the rise. Political radicalism increased, as well as the resort to violence and the temptation to turn to authoritarian methods to handle internal problems.
—Nationalism was taking on anti-U. S. overtones.
—Other Western Hemisphere nations seriously questioned whether our assistance, trade and investment policies would match the realities of the 1970's.

Toward a Policy for the 1970's

From the outset, the Administration recognized the need to redefine the special concern of the United States for the nations of the hemisphere. We were determined to reflect the forces of change in our approach and in our actions.

We approached this task in two phases: First, we sought to appraise the state of the hemisphere, to analyze the problems that existed, and to determine fundamental policy objectives; then, we expressed our conclusions in specific policies and programs.

To get a fresh perspective, early in my Administration I asked Governor Nelson A. Rockefeller to undertake a fact-finding mission throughout the region. His conclusions and recommendations, together with other government studies, were intensively reviewed by the NSC during the summer and early fall. This review addressed some of the basic questions: whether we should continue to have a "special relationship;" if so, what its essential purpose and substance ought to be and how best to achieve it.

We concluded that:

—A "special relationship" with Latin American has existed historically, and there are compelling reasons to maintain and strengthen our ties.
—The goal of such a relationship today should be to create a community of independent, self-reliant states linked together in a vital and useful association.
—United States assistance to its neighbors is an essential part of that relationship.
—The United States should contribute, not dominate. We alone cannot assume the responsibility for the economic and social development of other nations. This is a process deeply rooted in each nation's history and evolution. Responsibility has to be shared for progress to be real.
—For the 70's, we therefore had to shape a relationship that would encourage other nations to help themselves. As elsewhere in the world, our basic role is to persuade and supplement, not to prescribe. Each nation must be true to its own character.

On October 31, I proposed a new partnership in the Americas to reflect these concepts, a partnership in which all voices are heard and none is predominant. I outlined the five basic principles governing this new approach:

"First, a firm commitment to the inter-American system, to the compacts which bind us in that system—as exemplified by the Organization of American States and by the principles so nobly set forth in its charter.
"Second, respect for national identity and national dig-

nity, in a partnership in which rights and responsibilities are shared by a community of independent states.

"Third, a firm commitment to continued United States assistance for hemispheric developments.

"Fourth, a belief that the principal future pattern of this assistance must be U.S. support for Latin American initatives, and that this can best be achieved on a multilateral basis within the inter-American system.

"Finally, a dedication to improving the quality of life in this new world of ours—to making people the center of our concerns, and to helping meet their economic, social and human needs."

In this speech we also began laying the foundations of an action program for progress. These are actions that reflect our new approach of enabling other Western Hemisphere nations to help themselves. And they are actions that can realistically be implemented. I refused to propose grandiose spending programs that had no prospect of Congressional approval, or to make promises that could not be fulfilled.

A less than realistic approach would have blunted our partners' sense of participation and generated false hopes. The time for dependency and slogans was over. The time for partnership and action was at hand.

Action

We are shaping programs together with the other nations of the Western Hemisphere, not devising them on our own. And where we once relied on bilateral exchanges, we are turning more to multilateral groups.

One of the principal cooperative forums is the Inter-American Economic and Social Council, the economic and development channel of the Organization for American States. Shortly after my speech, and again early this year, this body met to consider our proposals and those of our friends. In these continuing meetings and in other multilateral exchanges we are putting forward our suggestions for give-and-take discussions.

We have made realistic action proposals to meet specific objectives:

—*Share Responsibility.* To insure that the shaping of the Western Hemisphere's future reflects the will of the other nations of this hemisphere, I affirmed the need for a fundamental change in the way we manage development assistance. I proposed that the nations of the hemisphere evolve an effective multilateral mechanism for bilateral assistance. The precise form this takes will be worked out with our partners. IA-ECOSOC has directed the Inter-American Committee for the Alliance for Progress (CIAP) and the Inter-American Bank to explore ways to increase their participation in development decisions. The goal is to enable the other Western Hemisphere nations to assume a primary role in setting priorities within the hemisphere, developing realistic programs and keeping their own performance under critical review. To demonstrate United States interest in improving and strengthening our multilateral institutions, I authorized financial support—totaling $23 million in grant funds—to strengthen the activities of CIAP and the Inter-American Bank. I also authorized our representatives to agree to submit to CIAP, for its review, United States economic and financial programs as they affect the other nations of the hemisphere. Similar reviews are made of the other hemisphere countries' policies, but the United States had not, prior to this decision, opened its policies to such a consultation.

—*Expand Trade.* To help other Western Hemisphere nations to increase their export earnings and thus contribute to balanced development and economic growth, I have committed the United States to a program which would help these countries improve their access to the expanding markets of the industrialized world:

—• The U.S. will press for a liberal system of generalized tariff preferences for all developing countries. We are working toward a system that would eliminate discriminations against South American exports that exist in other countries. Through the Organization for Economic Cooperation and Development and the United Nations Conference on Trade and Development, we are pressing other developed nations to recognize the need for a genuinely progressive tariff preference system.

—• I committed the U.S. to lead an effort to reduce non-tariff barriers to trade maintained by nearly all

industrialized countries. We seek to lead a concerted multilateral reduction in non-tariff barriers on products of major interest to South America, taking advantage of the work going on in the General Agreement on Tariffs and Trade.
—● I pledged to support increased technical and financial assistance to promote Latin American trade expansion.
—● I promised to support the establishment within the inter-American system of regular procedures for advance consultations on all trade matters, and we proposed specific mechanisms for this purpose. In early February, IA-ECOSOC agreed to establish a standing special committee which will meet regularly for consultation on mutual economic problems, including trade and development.

—*Ease AID restrictions.* To make development assistance more helpful and effective, we are taking several actions:
—● I ordered that from November 1, all loan dollars sent to Latin America under AID be freed to allow purchases not only in the U.S. but anywhere in Latin America. This partial "untying" of our assistance loans removed restrictions that had burdened borrowers and promised to provide an incentive for industrial development in its region.
—● We have removed a number of other procedural restrictions on the use of AID funds. We eliminated, for example, the requirement under which recipient countries were forced to import U.S. goods they would not have imported under normal trade conditions—the "additionality" provision.
—● The Peterson Task Force (which is studying our overall assistance Programs) is reviewing other procedural and administrative restrictions. We aim to streamline our lending and make it more effective.

—*Assure Special Representation.* To reflect our special concern for this region, I proposed establishing the position of Under Secretary of State for Western Hemisphere Affairs. The new Under Secretary will be given authority to coordinate all of our activities in this region. On December 20 the Secretary of State submitted implementing legislation to Congress.

—*Support Regionalism.* To encourage regional cooperation we have offered to support economic integration efforts. We have reiterated our offer of financial assistance to the Central American Common Market, the Caribbean

Free Trade Area, the Andean Group and to an eventual Latin American Common Market.

—*Ease Debt Burdens.* To help nations heavily burdened by large debts and their servicing we have urged the Inter-American Committee for the Alliance for Progress (CIAP) to join us in approaching other creditor nations and international lending agencies to study these problems. In February the IA-ECOSOC authorized CIAP to proceed along this line. As members of CIAP we have offered our full cooperation and expressed our willingness to join in an approach to other creditor nations.

—*Share Science and Technology.* To help turn science to the service of the hemisphere:

—● We will contribute to the support and financing of initiatives in these fields, including research and development, regional training centers, and transfer of technology.
—● We are developing a program for training and orientation of Latin American specialists in the field of scientific and technical information.
—● The OAS will sponsor a conference next year on the application of science and technology to Latin America.

This is the beginning of action for progress. But it is only a beginning. There is a long way to go.

Agenda for the Future

During the 1970's the nations of this hemisphere will continue to experience profound change in their societies and institutions. Aspirations rise while the intensity and complexity of social and economic problems increase, and most American governments must straddle the widening gap between demands and resources. If these governments cannot find greater resources, their prospects for solving their problems through rational policies will fade. The results will be more instability, more political radicalism, more of the wrong kind of nationalism.

This is the dilemma which the hemisphere faces in the 1970's. It prompted the efforts made by the hemisphere nations to forge new development and trade policies in the series of meetings of the Inter-American Economic and

Social Council during the latter half of 1969. Against this backdrop our friends will seek our cooperation, judge the credibility of our words, and measure the value of our actions.

In practical terms, we shall confront increased pressures:

—For capital resources to finance development and reform. We shall have to find ways to achieve adequate levels of resources, to use them more effectively and to transfer them through improved institutions and channels. We believe we can meet these needs through partnership, with shared responsiblity for development decisions and major efforts by the United States and other developed nations.

—For growing markets to expand exports. We shall have to face frankly the contradictions we will find between our broader foreign policy interests and our more particular domestic interests. Unless we can demonstrate to our sister nations evidence of our sincerity and of our help in this area while recognizing practical constraints, we cannot achieve the effective partnership we seek. A liberal trade policy that can support development is necessary to sustain a harmonious hemispheric system.

—Against foreign investments. Foreign investments are the most exposed targets of frustration, irrational politics, misguided nationalism. Their potential for mutual benefits will only be realized through mutual perception and tact. The nations of this hemisphere must work out arrangements which can attract the needed technical and financial resources of foreign investment. For their part, investors must recognize the national sensitivities and political needs of the 1970's. There is no more delicate task than finding new modes which permit the flow of needed investment capital without a challenge to national pride and prerogative.

There will be political and diplomatic pressures as well. The Inter-American community will have to consider:

—how to maintain peace in the face of border disputes and neighbors' quarrels;
—how to meet the problems of subversive threats to internal security and order;

—how to handle legitimate desires to modernize security forces without starting arms races;

—how to view internal political instabilities and extra-legal changes of government among us.

In both the development and security spheres we shall have to adapt the formalities of the inter-American system to rapidly changing realities. An amended OAS charter will very soon take effect. We shall need to work to enhance the effectiveness of its constituent organizations. Above all, our special partnership must accommodate the desire of the Latin Americans to consult among themselves and formulate positions which they can then discuss with us.

Within the broad commonality of our relationship, there is great diversity. In a period of such profound social and cultural change, emerging domestic structures will differ by country, reflecting various historical roots, particular contexts, and national priorities. We can anticipate different interpretations of reality, different conceptions of self-interest and different conclusions on how to resolve problems.

The United States must comprehend these phenomena. We must recognize national interests may indeed diverge from ours rather than merge. Our joint task is to construct a community of institutions and interests broad and resilient enough to accommodate our national divergencies. It is in this context that we are giving intensive study to Governor Rockefeller's recommendations for additional actions.

Our concepts of future American relations must thus be grounded in differences as well as similarities. Our mandate is to produce creativity from diversity. Our challenge is the vision I painted in my October 31 speech:

"Today, we share an historic opportunity.

"As we look together down the closing decades of this century, we see tasks that summon the very best that is in us. But those tasks are difficult precisely because they do mean the difference between despair and fulfillment for most of the 600 million people who will live in Latin

America by the year 2000. Those lives are our challenge. Those lives are our hope. And we could ask no prouder reward than to have our efforts crowned by peace, prosperity and dignity in the lives of those 600 million human beings, each so precious and each so unique—our children and our legacy."

Asia and the Pacific

"What we seek for Asia is a community of free nations able to go their own way and seek their own destiny with whatever cooperation we can provide—a community of independent Asian countries, each maintaining its own traditions and yet each developing through mutual cooperation. In such an arrangement, we stand ready to play a responsible role in accordance with our commitments and basic interests."

Statement by the President
at Bangkok, Thailand
July 28, 1969

Three times in a single generation, Americans have been called upon to cross the Pacific and fight in Asia. No region of the world has more engaged our energies in the postwar period. No continent has changed more rapidly or with greater complexity since World War II. Nowhere has the failure to create peace been more costly or led to greater sacrifice.

America's Asian policy for the 1970's must be based on the lessons of this sacrifice. Does it mean that the United States should withdraw from Asian affairs? If not, does it mean that we are condemned to a recurring cycle of crisis and war in a changing setting beyond the understanding or influence of outsiders?

Our answers to these questions provide the concepts behind this Administration's approach to Asia.

First, we remain involved in Asia. We are a Pacific power. We have learned that peace for us is much less likely if there is no peace in Asia.

Second, behind the headlines of strife and turmoil, the fact remains that no region contains a greater diversity of vital and gifted peoples, and thus a greater potential for cooperative enterprises. Constructive nationalism and economic progress since World War II have strengthened the new nations of Asia internally. A growing sense of Asian identity and concrete action toward Asian cooperation are creating a new and healthy pattern of international relationships in the region. Our Asian friends, especially Japan, are in a position to shoulder larger responsibilities for the peaceful progress of the area. Thus, despite its troubled past, Asia's future is rich in promise. That promise has been nurtured in part by America's participation.

Third, while we will maintain our interests in Asia and the commitments that flow from them, the changes taking place in that region enable us to change the character of our involvement. The responsibilities once borne by the United States at such great cost can now be shared. America *can* be effective in helping the peoples of Asia harness the forces of change to peaceful progress, and in supporting them as they defend themselves from those who would subvert this process and fling Asia again into conflict.

Our friends in Asia have understood and welcomed our concept of our role in that continent. Those with whom the Vice President, the Secretary of State and I spoke during our visits there agreed that this was the most effective way in which we can work together to meet the military challenges and economic opportunities of the new Asia.

Our new cooperative relationship concerns primarily two areas of challenge—military threats, and the great task of development.

Defense

Our important interests and those of our friends are still threatened by those nations which would exploit change and which proclaim hostility to the United States as one of the fundamental tenets of their policies. We do not assume that these nations will always remain hostile, and will work toward improved relationships wherever possible.

But we will not underestimate any threat to us or our allies, nor lightly base our present policies on untested assumptions about the future.

At the beginning of my trip last summer through Asia, I described at Guam the principles that underlie our cooperative approach to the defense of our common interests. In my speech on November 3, I summarized key elements of this approach.

> —The United States will keep all its treaty commitments.
> —We shall provide a shield if a nuclear power threatens the freedom of a nation allied with us, or of a nation whose survival we consider vital to our security and the security of the region as a whole.
> —In cases involving other types of aggression we shall furnish military and economic assistance when requested and as appropriate. But we shall look to the nation directly threatened to assume the primary responsibility of providing the manpower for its defense.

This approach requires our commitment to helping our partners develop their own strength. In doing so, we must strike a careful balance. If we do too little to help them—and erode their belief in our commitments—they may lose the necessary will to conduct their own self-defense or become disheartened about prospects of development. Yet, if we do too much, and American forces do what local forces can and should be doing, we promote dependence rather than independence.

In providing for a more responsible role for Asian nations in their own defense, the Nixon Doctrine means not only a more effective use of common resources, but also an American policy which can best be sustained over the long run.

Economic and Political Partnership

The partnership we seek involves not only defense. Its ultimate goal must be equally close cooperation over a much broader range of concerns—economic as well as political and military. For in that close cooperation with our Asian friends lies our mutual commitment to peace in Asia and the world.

Our goal must be particularly close cooperation for economic development. Here, too, our most effective contribution will be to support Asian initiatives in an Asian framework.

Our partnership will rest on the solid basis of Asia's own wealth of human and material resources. Acting jointly, its peoples offer each other a wide range of energy and genius. Their benefits shared, its land and products can overcome the unmet needs which have often sparked conflict. Already, the Republics of Korea and China, Thailand, Singapore and Malaysia can show a doubling of their gross national product in the last decade. Korea's annual growth rate of 15 per cent may be the highest in the world; the Republic of China, no longer an economic aid recipient, now conducts a technical assistance program of its own in 27 other countries.

Thus, the potential for cooperation among Asian countries is strong, and progress is already apparent. New multi-national organizations are sharing agricultural and technical skills. When the war in Vietnam is ended, reconstruction can be carried out in a regional context. And we look forward to continued cooperation with a regional effort to harness the power of the Mekong River.

The successful start of the Asian Development Bank, of which we are a member, illustrates the potential of Asian initiatives and regionalism. It is an *Asian* institution, with a requirement that the Bank's president, seven of its ten directors, and 60 per cent of its capital come from Asia.

Our hopes for Asia are thus for a continent of strong nations drawing together for their mutual benefit on their own terms, and creating a new relationship with the rest of the international community.

Japan, as one of the great industrial nations of the world, has a unique and essential role to play in the development of the new Asia. Our policy toward Japan during the past year demonstrates our conception of the creative partnership we seek with all Asian nations.

Upon entering office, I faced a pivotal question concerning the future of our relations with Japan: the status of Okinawa. What did we consider more important—the maintenance of American administration of Okinawa with no adjustments in the conditions under which we operate our bases, or the strengthening of our relationship with Japan over the long-term? We chose the second course because our cooperation with Japan will be crucial to our efforts to help other Asian nations develop in peace. Japan's partnership with us will be a key to the success of the Nixon Doctrine in Asia.

In November, I therefore agreed with Prime Minister Sato during his visit to Washington that we would proceed with arrangements for the return of Okinawa in 1972, with our bases remaining after its reversion in the same status as our bases in Japan. This was among the most important decisions I have taken as President.

For his part, Prime Minister Sato expressed the intention of the Japanese Government to expand and improve its aid programs in Asia in keeping with the economic growth of Japan. He agreed with me that attention to the economic needs of the developing countries was essential to the development of international peace and stability. He stated Japan's intention to accelerate the reduction and removal of its restrictions on trade and capital. He also stated that Japan was exploring what it could do to bring about stability and reconstruction in postwar Southeast Asia. The Prime Minister affirmed that it is in Japan's interest that we carry out fully our defensive commitments in East Asia.

We have thereby laid the foundation for US-Japanese cooperation in the 1970's.

Elsewhere, too, we have seen developments encouraging for the future of Asia. In Indonesia—which is virtually half of Southeast Asia—we have participated in multilateral efforts, aimed at achieving economic stability, which have already contributed much to the building of a prospering and peaceful nation.

The United States has a similar long-run interest in cooperation for progress in South Asia. The one-fifth of mankind who live in India and Pakistan can make the difference for the future of Asia. If their nation-building surmounts the centrifugal forces that have historically divided the subcontinent, if their economic growth keeps pace with popular demands, and if they can avert further costly rivalry between themselves, India and Pakistan can contribute their vast energies to the structure of a stable peace. But these are formidable "ifs." We stand ready to help the subcontinent overcome them. These nations' potential contribution to peace is too great for us to do otherwise.

Like the rest of Asia, India and Pakistan have changed significantly over the past decade. They have registered steady economic progress in many areas, and established a hopeful precedent for mutual cooperation in the Indus development scheme. Yet in the same period, each has felt the strains of continuing tension in their relations and their old bitter dispute flared again in brief warfare in 1965.

They have reordered their international relationships with East and West; each remains staunchly independent.

Over the next decade India, Pakistan, and their friends have an opportunity to build substantially on the constructive elements in this record, and above all, to work together to avert further wasteful and dangerous conflict in the area.

While I was in South Asia, I stated our view of the method and purpose of our economic assistance to Asia. These words were spoken in Pakistan, but they express our goals as well for India and all of Asia:

"I wish to communicate my Government's conviction that Asian hands must shape the Asian future. This is true, for example, with respect to economic aid, for it must be related to the total pattern of a nation's life. It must support the unique aspirations of each people. Its purpose is to encourage self-reliance, not dependence."

Issues for the Future

The fostering of self-reliance is the new purpose and direction of American involvement in Asia. But we are only at the beginning of a new road. However clear our conception of where we wish to go, we must be under no illusion that any policy can provide easy answers to the hard, specific issues which will confront us in Asia in coming years.

—While we have established general guidelines on American responses to Asian conflicts, in practice the specific circumstances of each case require careful study. Even with careful planning, we will always have to consider a basic and delicate choice. If we limit our own involvement in the interest of encouraging local self-reliance, and the threat turns out to have been more serious than we had judged, we will only have created still more dangerous choices. On the other hand, if we become unwisely involved, we risk stifling the local contribution which is the key to our long-run commitment to Asia.

—The success of our Asian policy depends not only on the strength of our partnership with our Asian friends, but also on our relations with Mainland China and the Soviet Union. We have no desire to impose our own prescriptions for relationships in Asia. We have described in the Nixon Doctrine our conception of our relations with Asian nations. We hope that other great powers will act in a similar spirit and not seek hegemony.

—Just as we and our allies have an interest in averting great power dominance over Asia, we believe that peace in the world would be endangered by great power conflict there—whether it involves us or not. This characterizes our attitude towards the Sino-Soviet dispute.

—Asian regional cooperation is at its beginning. We will confront subtle decisions as we seek to help maintain its momentum without supplanting Asian direction of the effort.

—A sound relationship with Japan is crucial in our common effort to secure peace, security, and a rising living standard in the Pacific area. We look forward to extending the cooperative relationship we deepened in 1969. But we shall not ask Japan to assume responsibilities inconsistent with the deeply felt concerns of its people.

—In South Asia, our good relations with India and Pakistan should not obscure the concrete dilemmas we will face. How can we bring home to both, for example, our serious concern over the waste of their limited resources in an arms race, yet recognize their legitimate interests in self-defense?

All these issues will confront this Administration with varying intensity over the coming years. We are planning now to meet challenges and anticipate crises. Our purpose in 1969 has been to make sure none was ignored or underestimated. The task ahead—for Asians and Americans—is to address all these issues with the imagination, realism and boldness their solutions demand if lasting peace is to come to Asia.

Vietnam

> "The people of Vietnam, North and South alike, have demonstrated heroism enough to last a century. And I speak from personal observation. I have been to North Vietnam, to Hanoi, in 1953, and all over South Vietnam. I have seen the people of the North and the people of the South. The people of Vietnam, North and South, have endured an unspeakable weight of suffering for a generation. And they deserve a better future."
>
> The President's Address to the 24th Session of the UN General Assembly, September 18, 1969

A just peace in Vietnam has been, and remains, our goal.

The real issues are the nature of that peace and how to achieve it. In addressing these issues at the beginning of my Administration, I had to consider the great consequences of our decisions.

I stated the consequences of a precipitate withdrawal in these terms in my speech of May 14:

> "When we assumed the burden of helping defend South Vietnam, millions of South Vietnamese men, women and children placed their trust in us. To abandon them now would risk a massacre that would shock and dismay everyone in the world who values human life.
>
> "Abandoning the South Vietnamese people, however,

would jeopardize more than lives in South Vietnam. It would threaten our long-term hopes for peace in the world. A great nation cannot renege on its pledges. A great nation must be worthy of trust.

"When it comes to maintaining peace, 'prestige' is not an empty word. I am not speaking of false pride or bravado—they should have no place in our policies. I speak, rather, of the respect that one nation has for another's integrity in defending its principles and meeting its obligations.

"If we simply abandoned our effort in Vietnam, the cause of peace might not survive the damage that would be done to other nations' confidence in our reliability.

"Another reason for not withdrawing unilaterally stems from debates within the Communist world ... If Hanoi were to succeed in taking over South Vietnam by force—even after the power of the United States had been engaged—it would greatly strengthen those leaders who scorn negotiation, who advocate aggression, who minimize the risks of confrontation with the United States. It would bring peace now but it would enormously increase the danger of a bigger war later."

My trip through Asia last summer made this fact more vivid to me than ever. I did not meet a single Asian leader who urged a precipitate U.S. withdrawal. The closer their nations were to the battlefield, the greater was their concern that America meet its responsibilities in Vietnam.

Less attention had been given to another important consequence of our decisions—within the United States itself. When the Administration took office, Vietnam had already led to a profound national debate. In considering our objectives there, I could only conclude that the peace must not intensify the bitter recrimination and divisions which the war had already inflicted on American society. Were we to purchase peace in Vietnam at the expense of greater suffering later, the American people would inevitably lose confidence in their leaders—not just in the Presidency or in either political party, but in the whole structure of American leadership.

For all these reasons, I resolved to seek a peace which all Americans could support, a peace in which all parties to the conflict would have a stake. I resolved also to be completely candid with the American public and Congress in presenting our policies, except for some details on matters of great sensitivity. I was determined to report the setbacks as well as achievements, the uncertainties as well as the hopeful signs.

To seek a just peace, we pursued two distinct but mutually supporting courses of action: Negotiations and Vietnamization. We want to achieve an early and fair settlement through negotiations. But if the other side refuses, we shall proceed to strengthen the South Vietnamese forces. This will allow us to replace our troops on an orderly timetable. We hope that as Vietnamization proceeds the Government of North Vietnam will realize that it has more to gain in negotiations than in continued fighting.

We do not pretend that our goals in Vietnam have been accomplished, or that the way ahead will be easy.

—In South Vietnam, we have helped the South Vietnamese make progress in increasing their defense capacity, and we have reduced the number of American men and casualties. Yet Vietnamization is still a developing process, and enemy intentions on the battlefield are unclear.
—At the conference table, we have made generous and reasonable proposals for a settlement. Yet the other side still refuses to negotiate seriously.

Despite these uncertainties, I believe that we are on the right road, and that we are moving toward our goals.

Negotiations

In seeking a negotiated settlement of the war, we did not underestimate the difficulties ahead:

—We knew that the basic questions at issue in negotiations—particularly the resolution of political power in such a war—were enormously complex. There could be no rigid formula or strict agenda.
—We were aware that Hanoi's actions and doctrinal statements about "protracted conflict," caused it to view nego-

tiations as a means of pressure, rather than as an avenue to a fair compromise.

—We realized that our opponent had sacrificed heavily; he had demonstrated a tenacious commitment to the war, and obviously harbored a deep mistrust of negotiations as a means of settling disputes. As I wrote to the late President Ho Chi Minh last July in an appeal to him to join us in finding a rapid solution: "It is difficult to communicate meaningfully across the gulf of four years of war."

These were formidable obstacles. But we were equally convinced that negotiations offered the best hope of a rapid settlement of the war. The specific issues were complex but could be resolved, once both sides made the fundamental decision to negotiate in a spirit of good-will. Therefore we and the Government of the Republic of Vietnam moved to demonstrate to a mistrustful adversary our willingness to negotiate seriously and flexibly.

On May 14 I made a number of far-reaching proposals for a settlement. They included a mutual withdrawal of all non-South Vietnamese forces from South Vietnam and internationally-supervised free elections.

I also indicated that we seek no bases in Vietnam and no military ties, that we are willing to agree to neutrality or to unification of Vietnam if that is what the South Vietnamese people choose.

In order to encourage the other side to negotiate, I indicated that our proposals were flexible, and that we were prepared to consider other approaches consistent with our principles. We insisted only on one general proposition for which the Government of North Vietnam itself has claimed to be fighting—that the people of South Vietnam be able to decide their own future free of outside interference.

The proposals I made on May 14 still stand. They offer all parties an opportunity to end the war quickly and on an equitable basis.

In a similar spirit, President Thieu of the Republic of Vietnam on July 11 offered a comprehensive set of proposals. They include free elections in which all the people and parties of South Vietnam can participate, including the National Liberation Front and its adherents, and a mixed Electoral Commission on which all parties can be represented. We have supported those proposals.

At Midway, in early June, President Thieu and I both publicly pledged to accept *any* outcome of free elections, regardless of what changes they might bring.

Throughout the year, we explored every means of engaging the other side in serious negotiations—in the public talks in Paris, in private conversations, and through reliable third parties.

To demonstrate our willingness to wind down the war, I also ordered a reduction in the level of our military operations in Vietnam. Our tactical air and B-52 operations have been reduced by over 25 per cent. Our combat deaths have dropped by two-thirds.

Nor were our proposals put forward on a take-it-or-leave-it basis. We have repeatedly expressed our willingness to discuss the other side's ten-point program. But Hanoi has adamantly refused even to discuss our proposals. It has refused to negotiate with the Government of the Republic of Vietnam, although it had agreed to do so as one of the "understandings" that led to the bombing halt. It has insisted that we must unconditionally and totally accept its demands for unilateral U.S. withdrawal and for the removal of the leaders of the Government of South Vietnam. It has demanded these things as conditions for just *beginning* negotiations. If we were to accept these demands, we would have conceded the fundamental points at issue. There would be nothing left to negotiate.

If the other side is interested in genuine negotiations there are many ways they can let us know and there are many channels open to them.

The key to peace lies in Hanoi—in its decision to end the bloodshed and to negotiate in the true sense of the word.

The United States has taken three major steps which we were told repeatedly would lead to serious negotiations. We stopped the bombing of North Vietnam; we began the withdrawal of U.S. forces from Vietnam; and we agreed to negotiate with the National Liberation Front as one of the parties to the negotiation. But none of those moves brought about the response or the reaction which their advocates had claimed. It is time for Hanoi to heed the concern of mankind and turn our negotiations into a serious give-and-take. Hanoi will find us forthcoming and flexible.

Vietnamization

The other course of action we are pursuing—Vietnamization—is a program to strengthen the ability of the South Vietnamese Government and people to defend themselves. It emphasizes progress in providing physical security for the Vietnamese people and in extending the authority of the South Vietnamese Government throughout the countryside.

Vietnamization is not a substitute for negotiations, but a spur to negotiations. In strengthening the capability of the Government and people of South Vietnam to defend themselves, we provide Hanoi with an authentic incentive to negotiate seriously now. Confronted by Vietnamization, Hanoi's alternative to a reasonable settlement is to continue its costly sacrifices while its bargaining power diminishes.

Vietnamization has two principal components. The first is the strengthening of the armed forces of the South Vietnamese in numbers, equipment, leadership and combat skills, and overall capability. The second component is the extension of the pacification program in South Vietnam.

Tangible progress has been made toward strengthening the South Vietnamese armed forces. Their number has grown, particularly the local and territorial forces. For example the numerical strength of the South Vietnamese Regional Forces and Popular Forces—important elements in resisting guerrilla attacks—has grown by more than 75,000 in the last year. The effectiveness of these forces is improving in most areas. In addition, about 400,000 weapons have been supplied to South Vietnamese villagers who have become part of the Peoples' Self Defense Force, a local militia.

Under the Vietnamization program, we have reversed the trend of American military engagement in Vietnam and the South Vietnamese have assumed a greater role in combat operations. We have cut the authorized strength of American forces by 115,500 as of April 15, 1970. American forces will continue to be withdrawn in accordance with an orderly schedule based on three criteria: the level of enemy activity; progress in the negotiations; and the increasing ability of the South Vietnamese people to assume for themselves the task of their own defense.

During this process, we have kept in close consultations with the allied nations—Australia, Korea, New Zealand, and Thailand—which also contribute troops to assist the Vietnamese. Their forces continue to bear a significant burden in this common struggle.

As the Vietnamese government bears the growing cost of these augmented forces, and as U.S. military spending in Vietnam is reduced with the continuing reduction of the U.S. military presence there, there will be additional strains on the Vietnamese economy. The Vietnamese will require assistance in dealing with these economic problems. Although our spending for purely military purposes in Vietnam can be expected to decrease substantially during the process of Vietnamization, some increases in our spending for economic purposes will be required.

Vietnamization also involves expansion of the pacification program. Our understanding of the pacification program and of the criteria for measuring its success needed improvement. I therefore ordered a comprehensive study of conditions in the countryside by a committee charged with analyzing the statistics of Vietnam and keeping the situation under constant review.

The study has concluded that the most meaningful criteria for South Vietnamese Government success in the countryside are the establishment in each hamlet of (1) an adequate defense, and (2) a fully functioning government resident in the hamlet 24 hours a day. If the Government can achieve these two objectives, it can prevent the enemy from subverting and terrorizing the population or mobilizing it for its own purposes. The enemy will be denied any but the most limited and furtive access to the people, and will encounter increasing hostility or indifference as they seek the assistance they formerly enjoyed. The enemy forces will be isolated and forced to fight as a conventional expeditionary force, being dependent on external sources of supply and reinforcement.

This is very important: Enemy main force activities have in the past relied on active assistance from the population in the countryside for intelligence, food, money and manpower. This has enabled the enemy to use the countryside as a springboard from which to strike at key Vietnamese cities and installations. If they are forced to fight as a conventional army, with their support provided from their own resources rather than from the population, the enemy will lose momentum as they move forward because their supply lines will lengthen and they will encounter increasing opposition.

To date, the pacification program is succeeding.

Enemy forces have suffered heavy casualties, many in the course of their own offensives of 1968 and early 1969. The operations of U.S. and South Vietnamese troops against enemy main force units have prevented those units from moving freely through the populated areas and have more and more forced them back into bases in remote areas and along the borders of South Vietnam.

Since 1967, the percentage of the rural population living in areas with adequate defense and a fully functioning local government—the two criteria for government success mentioned above—has more than doubled. By a similar standard, Viet Cong control over the rural population has dropped sharply to less than ten per cent.

The enemy is facing greater difficulty in recruitment and supply. North Vietnamese fillers are being used to bolster Viet Cong main force and local force units, whose strength appears to be declining in most areas. More of the enemy's time is taken up in gaining strength for new offensives which appear to be progressively less efficient.

* * * * * *

Claims of progress in Vietnam have been frequent during the course of our involvement there—and have often proved too optimistic. However careful our planning, and however hopeful we are for the progress of these plans, we are conscious of two basic facts.

—We cannot try to fool the enemy, who knows what is actually happening.
—Nor must we fool ourselves. The American people must have the full truth. We cannot afford a loss of confidence in our judgment and in our leadership.

Because the prospects and the progress of Vietnamization demand the most careful study and thoughtful analysis—by ourselves and our critics alike—we have made major efforts to determine the facts.

At my request, Secretary Laird and the Chairman of the Joint Chiefs of Staff, General Wheeler, have just traveled to Vietnam to look into the situation. Last fall, I asked Sir Robert Thompson, an objective British expert with long experience in the area, to make his own candid and independent appraisal for me.

We have established a Vietnam Special Studies Group whose membership includes my Assistant for National Security Affairs as Chairman, the Under Secretary of State, the Deputy Secretary of Defense, the Director of Central Intelligence, and the Chairman of the Joint Chiefs of Staff. I have directed this group to:

—sponsor and direct on a continuous basis systematic analyses of U.S. programs and activities in Vietnam;
—undertake special analytical studies on a priority basis as required to support broad policy and related programs decisions; and
—provide a forum for and encourage systematic interagency analysis of U.S. activities in Vietnam.

Essentially the purpose of this group is to direct studies of the factual situation in Vietnam. These studies are undertaken by analysts and individuals with experience in Vietnam drawn from throughout the government. Their findings are presented to the Vietnam Special Studies Group and the National Security Council.

As described below, the group has helped us identify problems for the future. It has provoked the most searching questions, as well as measured the progress we have achieved.

Prisoners of War

In human terms, no other aspect of conflict in Vietnam more deeply troubles thousands of American families than the refusal of North Vietnam to agree to humane treatment of prisoners of war or to provide information about men missing in action. Over 1400 Americans are now listed as missing or captured, some as long as five years, most with no word ever to their families. In the Paris meetings, we have sought repeatedly to raise this subject—to no avail. Far from agreeing to arrangements for the release of prisoners, the other side has failed even to live up to the humane standards of the 1949 Geneva Convention on prisoners of war: the provision of information about all prisoners, the right of all prisoners to correspond with their families and to receive packages, inspection of POW camps by an impartial organization such as the International Red Cross, and the early release of seriously sick and wounded prisoners.

This is not a political or military issue, but a matter of basic humanity. There may be disagreement about other aspects of this conflict, but there can be no disagreement on humane treatment for prisoners of war. I state again our readiness to proceed at once to arrangements for the release of prisoners of war on both sides.

Tasks for the Future

This Administration is carrying out a concerted and coordinated plan for peace in Vietnam. But the following tasks still remain:

—*Negotiations.* One task is to persuade the North Vietnamese Government to join us in genuine negotiations leading toward a compromise settlement which would assure the self-determination of the South Vietnamese people and would also ensure the continued neutrality of Laos. The fact that it has not yet given any indication of doing so does not necessarily mean that such a decision cannot come at any point. While we harbor no undue optimism, the history of negotiations on Vietnam shows that breakthroughs have always come with little warning after long deadlocks.

Hanoi faces serious and complicated issues in making the fundamental decision to seek a genuine settlement. Allied military pressures, uncertainties in its international support, strains within North Vietnam, the recent display of American public support for a just peace, and the strengthening of the South Vietnamese Government under Vietnamization, all argue for seeking a settlement now. On the other hand, Hanoi's mistrust of our intentions before and after a settlement, its hope that American domestic pressures will force us to withdraw rapidly or make major concessions, its hope for political instability and collapse in South Vietnam, its emotional commitment to the struggle, and its own political weakness in the South must weigh heavily against its willingness to negotiate.

We do not know what choice the North Vietnamese Government will make. For our part, we shall continue to try to make clear to that government that its true long-range interests lie in the direction of negotiations. As we have often said, we shall be flexible and generous when serious negotiations start at last.

—*Enemy Intentions.* Another crucial task is to evaluate Hanoi's intentions on the battlefield. We hope that the level of combat can be further reduced, but we must be prepared for new enemy offensives. The Government of North Vietnam could make no greater mistake than to assume that an increase in violence would be to its advantage. As I said on November 3, and have repeated since, if I conclude that increased enemy action jeopardizes our remaining forces in Vietnam, I will not hesitate to take strong and effective measures to deal with that situation.

—*Vietnamization.* A major problem we must face is whether the Vietnamization program will succeed. The enemy is determined and able, and will continue to fight unless he can be persuaded that negotiation is the best solution. The success of Vietnamization is a basic element in Hanoi's assessment of its policies, just as it is in our own.

—We are now attempting to determine the depth and durability of the progress which has been made in Vietnam. We are studying the extent to which it has been dependent on the presence of American combat and support forces as well as on expanded and improved South Vietnamese army and territorial forces. We are asking searching questions:

— • What is the enemy's capability to mount sustained operations? Could they succeed in undoing our gains?
— • What is the actual extent of improvement in Allied capabilities? In particular, are the Vietnamese developing the leadership, logistics capabilities, tactical know-how, and sensitivity to the needs of their own people which are indispensable to continued success?
— • What alternative strategies are open to the enemy in the face of continued allied success? If they choose to conduct a protracted, low-intensity war, could they simply wait out U.S. withdrawals and then through reinvigorated efforts, seize the initiative again and defeat the South Vietnamese forces?
— • Most important, what are the attitudes of the Vietnamese people, whose free choice we are fighting to preserve? Are they truly being disaffected from the Viet Cong, or are they indifferent to both sides? What do their attitudes imply about the likelihood that the pacification gains will stick?

These studies are continuing, as are our studies of the enemy situation and options. I have made it clear that I want the Vietnam Special Studies Group and the other agencies of the U.S. Government to provide the fullest possible presentation of the facts, whatever their policy implications might be.

Our task is to continue to proceed carefully in the policy of Vietnamization, and to find the means which will best support our purpose of helping the South Vietnamese to strengthen themselves.

Even as the fighting continues in Vietnam, we must

plan for the transition from war to peace. Much has already been done to bring relief to suffering people, to reconstruct war-torn areas and to promote economic rehabilitation. We have been supporting those efforts. We shall continue to support them and we shall count on other nations to help.

I look forward to the day when I shall not have to report on the problems of ending a complex war but rather on the opportunities offered by a stable peace, when the men and nations who have fought so long and so hard will be reconciled.

I expressed my hope for the future of Vietnam when I spoke to the United Nations on September 18:

> "When the war ends, the United States will stand ready to help the people of Vietnam—all of them—in their tasks of renewal and reconstruction. And when peace comes at last to Vietnam, it can truly come with healing in its wings."

The Middle East

> "... a peace which speaks not only about the integrity of nations, but also for the integrity of individuals."
>
> Letter to the President of
> American Near East Refugee
> Aid, October 21, 1969
>
> "... the peace that is not simply one of words but one which both parties will have a vested interest in maintaining."
>
> Welcoming remarks to Prime
> Minister of Israel,
> September 25, 1969

These statements reflect some of my thoughts on the nature of the peace which must come to the Middle East. At the same time, this is an area with great resources and prospects for economic progress. It is the first region of developing nations that is near to meeting its capital needs from its own resources.

Yet this area presents one of the sternest tests of our

quest for peace through partnership and accommodation of interests. It combines intense local conflict with great power involvement. This combination is all the more dangerous because the outside powers' interests are greater than their control.

Beyond the area of conflict and beyond this era of conflict, the United States is challenged to find new relationships in helping all the people of the area marshal their resources to share in this progress.

The most important of the areas' conflicts, between Arabs and Israel, is still far from settlement. It has serious elements of intractability, but its importance requires all concerned to devote their energies to helping to resolve it or make it less dangerous.

Local passions in the Middle East run so deep that the parties in conflict are seldom amenable to outside advice or influence. Each side is convinced that vital interests are at stake which cannot be compromised.

—Israel, having lived so long before on a thin margin of security, sees territories occupied in 1967 as providing physical security more tangible than Arab commitments to live at peace—commitments whose nature would be tested only after Israel had relinquished the buffer of the territories.
—For the Arabs, a settlement negotiated directly with the Israelis would require recognition of Israel as a sovereign state even while Israeli troops still occupy territory taken in 1967 and while Arab refugees remain homeless.
—For both sides and for the international community, Jerusalem is a special problem involving not only the civil and political concerns of two states but the interests of three great world religions.

A powerful legacy of fear and mistrust must be overcome if the parties are to be willing to subject their interests and grievances to the procedure of compromise. Until then, no formula acceptable to both sides, and no neutral definition of "a fair and reasonable settlement," can get very far.

However, a settlement should still be sought.

This Administration continues to believe that the United Nations cease-fire resolutions define the minimal conditions that must prevail on the ground if a settlement is to be achieved. We have persistently urged the parties in the area as well as the other major powers to do all possible to restore observance of the cease-fire.

Once those minimal conditions exist, we believe a settlement can only be achieved through the give and take of negotiation by those involved, in an atmosphere of mutual willingness to compromise. That is why this Administration has pressed this view in a series of consultations with leaders from the Middle East both in Washington and in their capitals, in bilateral discussions with the outside powers most concerned, and in formal talks with the Soviet Union and in the Four Power forum at the United Nations. In the course of these discussions, we have advanced specific proposals—outlined by Secretary Rogers in his speech of December 9—for creating a framework for negotiation in accordance with the United Nations resolution of November 22, 1967. These have been written with the legitimate concerns of all parties firmly in mind. They were made in an effort to try to help begin the process of negotiation under UN Ambassador Jarring's auspices. Observing that the United States maintained friendly ties with both Arabs and Israelis, the Secretary of State said that to call for Israeli withdrawal as envisaged in the UN resolution without achieving agreement on peace would be partisan toward the Arabs, while calling on the Arabs to accept peace without Israeli withdrawal would be partisan toward Israel.

But the United States cannot be expected to assume responsibility alone for developing the terms of peace or for guaranteeing them. Others—in the Middle East and among the great powers—must participate in the search for compromise. Each nation concerned must be prepared to subordinate its special interests to the general interest in peace. In the Middle East, especially, everyone must participate in making the peace so all will have an interest in maintaining it.

We have not achieved as much as we had hoped twelve

months ago through the discussions with the Soviet Union or the Four Power talks. We have gone as far as we believe useful in making new proposals until there is a response from other parties. But we shall continue to participate in the dialogue so long as we can make a contribution.

If the Arab-Israeli conflict cannot be finally resolved, at least its scope must be contained and the direct engagement of the major powers limited. For this is a second dimension of the conflict in the Middle East—the rivalries and interests of the major powers themselves.

The interests of the great powers are involved in the contests between local forces, but we also have a common interest in avoiding a direct confrontation. One of the lessons of 1967 was that the local events and forces have a momentum of their own, and that conscious and serious effort is required for the major powers to resist being caught up in them.

In its communications to the Soviet Union and others, this Administration has made clear its opposition to steps which could have the effect of drawing the major powers more deeply into the Arab-Israeli conflict—steps that could only increase the dangers without advancing the prospects for peace.

The activity of the Soviet Union in the Middle East and the Mediterranean has increased in recent years. This has consequences that reach far beyond the Arab-Israeli question. The United States has long-standing obligations and relationships with a number of nations in the Middle East and its policy is to help them enhance their own integrity and freedom. This Administration has shown its readiness to work with the Soviet Union for peace and to work alongside the Soviet Union in cooperation with nations in the area in the pursuit of peace. But the United States would view any effort by the Soviet Union to seek predominance in the Middle East as a matter of grave concern.

I believe that the time has passed in which powerful nations can or should dictate the future to less powerful nations. The policy of this Administration is to help strengthen the freedom of other nations to determine their own futures. Any effort by an outside power to exploit local conflict for its own advantage or to seek a special position of its own would be contrary to that goal.

For these reasons, this Administration has not only pressed efforts to restore observance of the cease-fire and to help begin the process of negotiating a genuine peace. It has also urged an agreement to limit the shipment of arms to the Middle East as a step which could help stabilize the situation in the absence of a settlement. In the meantime, however, I now reaffirm our stated intention to maintain careful watch on the balance of military forces and to provide arms to friendly states as the need arises.

This Administration clearly recognizes that the problem of the Middle East, rooted in a long history of local developments, will be solved only when the parties to the conflict—by reason or resignation—come to accommodate each others' basic, long-run interests. They must recognize that to do less will increasingly endanger everyone's basic goals.

Issues for the Future

We shall continue to seek to work together with all the region's nations, respecting their legitimate national interests and expecting that they will have the same regard for ours. But the emphasis must be on the word "together." The day is past when the large powers can or should be expected either to determine their course or to solve their problems for them. As the Secretary of State said on December 9:

> "[Peace] is . . . a matter of the attitudes and intentions of the parties. Are they ready to coexist with one another? Can a live-and-let-live attitude replace suspicion, mistrust and hate? A peace agreement between the parties must be based on clear and stated intentions and a willingness to bring about basic changes in the attitudes and conditions which are characteristic of the Middle East today."

The Middle East poses many challenges for the United States. First, of course, is the problem of resolving or containing major causes of conflict. No one should believe that a settlement even of the Arab-Israeli conflict would lead to the complete relaxation of tensions in the area. Other local rivalries and the turmoil accompanying social and economic change will continue to produce possibilities for conflict.

Yet, beyond that, a new problem faces us—the character of a constructive American relationship with an area with large capital resources of its own.

A number of nations in the area are well-launched toward economic modernization. Some of them have substantial revenues to finance this effort, and those that do not will increasingly rely on the efforts of nearby nations to help through regional funds. Large numbers of skilled technicians have been trained, and many of them have crossed borders to help neighbors.

This means that—while the United States will continue to help where it can—the need will decline for capital assistance and for the type of economic assistance which AID and its forerunners have provided. Of course, American technology, investment, education, managerial skills are still much in demand and can offer much in helping break bottlenecks that remain.

The challenge to the United States, therefore, is to find new tools—new programs, new legislation, new policies—that will permit our government and our citizens to relate productively to the first major area of the developing world to be close to meeting most of its capital needs from its own resources. We want to continue to work together. We must therefore—while persisting in the quest for peace—develop new relationships to meet the circumstances and demands of the 1970's.

Beyond the dangerous conflict of today, our vision of the Middle East is of a common effort by all those—the people of the area and friends outside—whose high purpose is to erase the scars of the past and to build a future consistent with their great heritage and abundant resources.

Africa

> "We know you have no easy task in seeking to assure a fair share of Africa's wealth to all her peoples. We know that the realization of equality and human dignity throughout the continent will be long and arduous in coming. But you can be sure as you pursue these difficult goals that the United States shares your hopes and your confidence in the future."
>
> President's Message
> to the Sixth Annual
> Assembly of the Organization
> of African Unity,
> September 6, 1969

In this greeting last September to the summit meeting of the Organization of African Unity, I expressed America's determination to support our African friends as they work to fulfill their continent's high promise. The unprecedented visit of the Secretary of State to Africa this month is a confirmation of this support.

One of the most dramatic and far-reaching changes of the last decade was the emergence of an independent Africa.

Only ten years ago, 32 countries covering nearly five-sixths of the Continent were still colonies, their voices silent in world affairs. Today, these are all sovereign nations, proudly determined to shape their own future. And contrary to fears so often voiced at their birth, these nations did not succumb to Communist subversion. Africa is one of the world's most striking examples, in fact, of the failure of the appeal of Communism in the new nations. African states now comprise one-third of the membership of the United Nations. African issues have become important moral and political questions. African views justly merit and receive the attention of the world.

But this rebirth of a continent has been hazardous as well as hopeful. Africa was the scene of many of the recurrent crises of the 1960's. There was the factional strife and international rivalry in the Congo, an arms race between Ethiopia and Somalia, the establishment of white minority rule in Southern Rhodesia, and the agonizing human loss in the Nigerian civil war.

The Continent still faces grave problems. The imbalances of economies and institutions once under full external control are only too evident today. Arbitrary boundaries drawn in European chancellories left many African countries vulnerable to tribal strife; and nowhere is the task of nation-building more taxing. Not least, Africans face the formidable task of strengthening their sense of identity and preserving traditional culture as their societies make the transition to modernity.

Over the last decade, America has not had a clear conception of its relationship with post-colonial Africa and its particular problems. Because of our traditional support of self-determination, and Africa's historic ties with so many of our own citizens, our sympathy and friendship for the new Africa were spontaneous. But without a coherent concept to structure our policies, we allowed ourselves to concentrate more on temporary crises than on their underlying causes. We expressed our support for Africa more by lofty phrases than by candid and constructive dialogue.

Just as we focus our policies elsewhere to meet a new era, we will be clear with ourselves and with our African friends on America's interests and role in the Continent. We have two major concerns regarding the future of Africa:

—That the Continent be free of great power rivalry or conflict in any form. This is even more in Africa's interest than in ours.
—That Africa realize its potential to become a healthy and prosperous region in the international community. Such an Africa would not only be a valuable economic partner for all regions, but would also have a greater stake in the maintenance of a durable world peace.

These interests will guide our policies toward the most demanding challenges facing Africa in the 1970's.

Development

The primary challenge facing the African Continent is economic development.

If the 1960's were years of high hopes and high rhetoric, the 1970's will have to be years of hard work and hard choices. The African nations and those who assist them must decide together on strict priorities in employing the relatively limited development capital available to the Continent. In doing this, Africa and its friends can benefit from several lessons of the past decade.

Certainly development will not always proceed as rapidly as the Africans and their friends hope. In many countries, needs will outrun local and international resources for some time. But solid and steady progress will be made if our common development investment concentrates on those basic if undramatic building blocks of economic growth—health, education, agriculture, transportation and local development. In particular, Africa will realize the full advantage of its own rich material resources only as it nurtures the wealth of its human resources. In close coordination with the Africans' own efforts, the United States will direct our aid at these fundamental building blocks.

Another lesson we have learned from the 1960's is the need for close regional cooperation, in order for Africa to get the most from development resources. The United States will work with other donors and the Africans to help realize the potential for cooperative efforts—by the support which we are giving, for example, to the East African Economic Community and the promising regional groupings in West Africa. We will recognize, however, that regional action is not the only road for African development. In some cases, for geographic or political reasons, it will not work.

Our assistance throughout the Continent will be flexible and imaginative. We will make a particular effort—including programs of technical assistance and new encouragement of private investment—to help those countries not in a position to participate in regional projects.

We have learned that there are no panaceas for African development. Each country faces its own problems and the solutions to them must spring from the national experience of each country. Foreign ideologies have often proven notoriously irrelevant, and even tragically wasteful, as designs for African progress. The most creative conceptual approaches to African development should come, of course, from the Africans themselves. Outsiders cannot prescribe the political framework most conducive to Africa's economic growth. In some countries, progress has depended upon stability. Yet elsewhere, solutions to local problems have been found amid periods of uncertainty or even turmoil.

The United States will measure African progress in terms of long-run social and economic accomplishment, and not in the political flux which is likely to accompany growth.

In Africa, as throughout the developing world, our goal in providing development aid is clear. We want the Africans to build a better life for themselves and their children. We want to see an Africa free of poverty and disease, and free too of economic or political dependence on any outside power. And we want Africans to build this future as *they* think best, because in that way both our help and their efforts will be most relevant to their needs.

As Secretary Rogers said in Ethiopia on February 12:

> "As a developed nation, we recognize a special obligation to assist in the economic development of Africa. Our resources and our capacity are not unlimited. We have many demands at home. We will, however, continue to seek the means, both directly and in cooperation with others, to contribute more effectively to economic development in Africa."

Nationhood

Africa's second challenge in the 1970's will be to weather the inevitable strains which will come with the further development of nations which house a great diversity of peoples and cultures.

We have witnessed tragic manifestations of this problem in the civil strife in the Congo and Nigeria. The progress of national integration may be stormy elsewhere.

Such turmoil presents a tempting target to forces outside Africa ready to exploit the problems of change to their own advantage. But foreign intervention, whatever its form or source, will not serve the long-run interests of the Africans themselves.

The United States approaches these problems of national integration with a policy which clearly recognizes the limits as well as the obligations of our partnership with Africa:

—We will not intervene in the internal affairs of African nations. We strongly support their right to be independent, and we will observe their right to deal with their own problems independently. We believe that the national integrity of African states must be respected.

—However, we will distinguish between non-interference politically and the humanitarian obligation to help lessen human suffering.

—Finally, consulting our own interests, we will help our friends in Africa to help themselves when they are threatened by outside forces attempting to subvert their independent development. It is another lesson of the 1960's, however, that African defense against subversion, like African development, must by borne most directly by Africans rather than by outsiders.

Southern Africa

The third challenge facing Africa is the deep-seated tension in the southern sixth of the Continent.

Clearly there is no question of the United States condoning, or acquiescing in, the racial policies of the white-ruled regimes. For moral as well as historical reasons, the United States stands firmly for the principles of racial equality and self-determination.

At the same time, the 1960's have shown all of us— Africa and her friends alike—that the racial problems in the southern region of the Continent will not be solved quickly. These tensions are deeply rooted in the history of the region, and thus in the psychology of both black and white.

These problems must be solved. But there remains a real issue in how best to achieve their resolution. Though we abhor the racial policies of the white regimes, we cannot agree that progressive change in Southern Africa is furthered by force. This history of the area shows all too starkly that violence and the counter-violence it inevitably provokes will only make more difficult the task of those on both sides working for progress on the racial question.

The United States warmly welcomes, therefore, the recent Lusaka Manifesto, a declaration by African leaders calling for a peaceful settlement of the tensions in Southern Africa. That statesmanlike document combines a commitment to human dignity with a perceptive understanding of the depth and complexity of the racial problem in the area—a combination which we hope will guide the policies of Africa and her friends as they seek practical policies to deal with this anguishing question.

Issues for the Future

American policy toward Africa, then, will illustrate our general approach to building an enduring peace. Our stake in the Continent will not rest on today's crisis, on political maneuvering for passing advantage, or on the strategic priority we assign it. Our goal is to help sustain the process by which Africa will gradually realize economic progress to match its aspirations.

We must understand, however, that this process is only beginning. Its specific course is unclear. Its success depends in part on how we and the Africans move now in the climate as well as the substance of our relations.

—Africa's friends must find a new tone of candor in their essential dialogue with the Continent. All too often over the past decade the United States and others have been guilty of telling proud young nations, in misguided condescension, only what we thought they wanted to hear. But I know from many talks with Africans, including two trips to the Continent in 1957 and 1967, that Africa's new leaders are pragmatic and practical as well as proud, realistic as well as idealistic. It will be a test of diplomacy for all concerned to face squarely common problems and differences of view. The United States will do all it can to establish this new dialogue.

—Most important, there must be new and broader forms of mobilizing the external resources for African development. The pattern of the multilateral consortium which in the past few years has aided Ghana should be employed more widely elsewhere. This will require the closest cooperation between the Africans and those who assist them. There is much to be gained also if we and others can help devise ways in which the more developed African states can share their resources with their African neighbors.

—The United States is firmly committed to non-interference in the Continent, but Africa's future depends also on the restraint of other great powers. No one should seek advantage from Africa's need for assistance, or from future instability. In his speech on February 12, Secretary Rogers affirmed that:

"We have deep respect for the independence of the African nations. We are not involved in their internal affairs. We want our relations with them to be on a basis of mutual respect, mutual trust and equality. We have no desire for any domination of any country or any area and have no desire for any special influence in Africa, except the influences that naturally and mutually develop among friends."

The Africa of the 1970's will need schools rather than sympathy, roads rather than rhetoric, farms rather than formulas, local development rather than lengthy sermons. We will do what we can in a spirit of constructive cooperation rather than by vague declarations of good will. The hard facts must be faced by Africans and their friends, and the hard work in every corner of the Continent must be done. A durable peace cannot be built if the nations of Africa are not true partners in the gathering prosperity and security which fortify that peace.

International Economic Policy

Peace has an economic dimension. In a world of independent states and interdependent economies, failure to collaborate is costly—in political as well as economic terms. Economic barriers block more than the free flow of goods and capital across national borders; they obstruct a more open world in which ideas and people, as well as goods and machinery, move among nations with maximum freedom.

Good U.S. economic policy is good U.S. foreign policy. The pre-eminent role that we play in the world economy gives us a special responsibility. In the economic sphere, more than in almost any other area, what we do has a tremendous impact on the rest of the world. Steady non-inflationary growth in our domestic economy will promote steady non-inflationary growth in the world as a whole. The stability of our dollar is essential to the stability of the world monetary system. Our continued support of a stronger world monetary system and freer trade is crucial to the expansion of world trade and investment on which the prosperity and development of most other countries depend.

As in other areas of foreign policy, our approach is a sharing of international responsibilities. Our foreign economic policy must be designed to serve our purpose of strengthening the ties that make partnership work.

We have an excellent foundation. In no other area of our foreign policy has the record of cooperation been so long and so successful. From the 1944 Bretton Woods Conference (which created the International Monetary Fund) and the 1947 General Agreement on Tariffs and Trade (which established a code for the orderly conduct of trade), to the Kennedy Round of tariff negotiations and the recent creation of Special Drawing Rights, free nations have worked together to build and strengthen a system of economic relationships. We derive strength from their strength; we collaborate for our common interest.

International Monetary Policy

International monetary matters pose most sharply the potential tug-of-war between interdependent economies and independent national policies. Each country's balance of payments encompasses the full range of its economic and political relations with other nations—trade, travel, investment, military spending, foreign aid. The international monetary system links these national payments positions, and hence the domestic economies of all countries. It thus lies at the heart of all international economic relations and it must function smoothly if world trade, international investment and political relations among nations are to prosper—particularly since imbalances inevitably arise as some countries temporarily spend more abroad than they earn, while others correspondingly earn more than they spend.

The system must include two elements:

—adequate supplies of internationally acceptable money and credit to finance payments imbalances among countries; and
—effective means through which national economies can adjust to one another to avoid the development of excessive and prolonged imbalances.

The inadequacies of both elements caused the recurring monetary crises of the 1960's.

An *adequate money supply* is needed internationally just as it is domestically. Shortages of internationally acceptable money induce national authorities to take hasty and often restrictive measures to protect their own monetary reserves, or to pull back from liberalization of trade and investment. Such actions clash with the objective of the international economic system, which precisely by freeing trade and capital, has helped promote the unparalleled prosperity of the postwar world. In short, an inadequate world money supply can hinder the pursuit of world prosperity which, in turn, can generate serious political problems among nations.

At the other extreme, excessive levels of world reserves could contribute to world inflation. They could permit countries to finance imbalances indefinitely, delaying too long the actions needed to adjust their own economies to those of their trading partners. Since failure to adjust may permit a country to drain resources away from the rest of the world, excessive levels of reserves can also generate serious political problems.

In 1969, the world took a step of profound importance by creating international money to help provide for adequate—neither too small nor too large—levels of world reserves. Through the International Monetary Fund, the United States joined with the other free nations to create, for an initial three-year period, almost $10 billion of Special Drawing Rights—a truly international money, backed by the entire community of free nations, created in amounts determined jointly by these nations, in recognition of the fact that a steadily growing world economy requires growing reserves.

There exist other types of internationally accepted money, particularly gold and dollars, which the world has previously relied upon and will continue to use. But it is clear that the relative role of gold must diminish. Our critical monetary arrangements must not rest on the vagaries of gold production. Nor should the world be forced to rely more heavily on dollars flowing from a U.S. payments deficit. This would appear to some as representing largely national determination of the international monetary supply, not wholly responsive to international needs. Moreover, prolonged deficits could jeopardize our own international financial position and cause concern about the stability of the dollar.

A truly international money was thus needed to meet a truly international problem. The nations of the world did not shrink from the bold innovation required to meet that need. As a result, the foundations of the world economy, and hence world stability, are far stronger today.

To be sure, the first creation of Special Drawing Rights does not by itself assure an adequate supply of internationally acceptable money. The international community will have to make periodic decisions on how many Special Drawing Rights to create. The relationship among the different types of international money—gold, dollars, and now Special Drawing Rights—could again cause problems. Most important, a steady economic performance by the United States will be necessary to maintain full international confidence in the dollar, whose stability remains crucial to the smooth functioning of the world economy. But we have gone a long way toward meeting the needs for an adequate supply of international money.

The second fundamental requirement of an international monetary system—*the mutual adjustment of national economies*—still calls for improvement. Imbalances among nations can only be financed temporarily. Constructive means must exist by which they can be rectified in an orderly way. Such adjustment should not require countries to resort to prolonged restrictions on international transactions, for this runs counter to the fundamental objective of an open world. Neither should it force countries to adopt internal economic policies, such as excessive rates of inflation or unemployment, which conflict with their national economic and social objectives. Both approaches have been adopted all too frequently in the past.

Improved means of adjustment are thus high on the agenda for the further development of the international monetary system in the 1970's. As economic interdependence accelerates, better coordination among national economies will become even more necessary. Such coordination must rest on a solid base of effective internal policies. For example, we in the United States must squarely face the fact that our inflation of the past five years—left unchecked—would not only undermine our domestic prosperity but jeopardize the effort to achieve better international equilibrium. We look forward to the results of the international discussions, already under way, examining the means through which exchange rates between national currencies might be adjusted so that such changes, when they become necessary, can take place more promptly and less disruptively.

In this environment, the remaining restrictions on international transactions can be steadily reduced. We will do our share. That intent was plain in the actions we took in 1969 to relax our restraints on capital outflows for U.S. corporations and banks and to eliminate the most onerous restrictions on our aid to developing countries.

Trade Policy

Freer trade among all nations provides greater economic benefits for each nation. It minimizes potential political frictions as well. These conclusions are truer today than ever before, as the growing interdependence of the world economy creates new opportunities for productive exchange.

But growing interdependence also means greater reliance by each nation on all other nations. Each is increasingly exposed to its trading partners. In today's world, all major countries must pursue freer trade if each country is to do so. The principle of true reciprocity must lie at the heart of trade policy—as it lies at the heart of all foreign policy.

In 1969, the United States took a series of steps toward dismantling trade barriers and assuring fair treatment for our own industry and agriculture in world commerce. I submitted new trade legislation which proposed:

—Elimination of the American Selling Price system of tariff valuation for certain chemicals and other products, which would bring us immediate trade concessions in Europe and elsewhere. Because it is seen by many abroad as our most important non-tariff barrier to trade, its elimination might also open the door to further reductions of barriers to U.S. exports.

—Improvement of the means to help U.S. industries, firms and workers adjust to import competition.

—Restoration of Presidential authority to reduce tariffs by a modest amount, when necessary to promote U.S. trade interests.

—New Presidential authority to retaliate against other countries if their trading practices unfairly impede our own exports in world markets.

We called on our trading partners to begin serious discussions on the remaining non-tariff barriers to trade, which have become even more important as tariff levels have been reduced.

We took specific steps toward easing economic relations between the United States and Communist China.

Finally, we proposed a liberal system of tariff preferences for exports of the developing countries.

This proposal is designed to meet one of the world's major economic and political problems—the struggle of the developing countries to achieve a satisfactory rate of economic development. Development can be promoted by aid, but aid cannot and should not be relied on to do the whole job. The low-income countries need increased export earnings to finance the imports they need for development. They need improved access for their products to the massive markets of the industrialized nations. Such export increases must come largely in manufactured goods, since the demand for most primary commodities—their traditional exports—grows relatively slowly. And these countries are at early stages of industrialization, so they face major hurdles in competing with the industrialized countries for sales of manufactured goods.

Against this background, we proposed that all industrialized nations eliminate their tariffs on most manufactured products exported to them by all developing countries. Such preferential treatment would free an important and rapidly growing part of the trade between these two groups of nations. It would therefore provide an important new impetus to world economic development.

The main tasks for the immediate future are to complete the actions started in 1969:

—Passage of this Administration's trade bill.
—Progress in the international discussions on non-tariff barriers and impediments to trade in agricultural products.
—Successful resolution of the negotiations on tariff preferences.

Beyond these steps lie new challenges for U.S. trade policy. I am establishing a Commission on International Trade and Investment Policy to help develop our approaches to them:

—*Trade and Investment.* Foreign investment, symbolized by the multinational corporation, has become increasingly important in relation to the flows of goods which have been the focus of traditional trade policy. We must explore more fully the relationship between our trade and foreign investment policies.

—*Trade Adjustment.* We must learn how better to adjust our own economy to the dynamic forces of world trade, so that we can pursue our objective of freer trade without unacceptable domestic disruption.

—*East-West Trade.* We look forward to the time when our relations with the Communist countries will have improved to the point where trade relations can increase between us.

—*The European Community.* We will watch with great interest the developing relations between the European Community and other nations, some of which have applied for membership. The Community's trade policies will be of increasing importance to our own trade policy in the years ahead.

International Assistance

The international economic successes of the past have been mainly among the industrial nations. The successes of the future must occur at least equally in the economic relations between the industrial nations and the developing world. These new achievements may not be as dramatic as the creation of the Common Market, or the completion of the Kennedy Round of trade negotiations, or the birth of Special Drawing Rights. But the needs are at least as compelling.

There will be a continued requirement for international assistance to developing countries. First, however, we must be clear about what aid can do and what it cannot do. If aid is to be effective, its function must be understood by both donor and recipient.

Economic assistance is not a panacea for international stability, for political development, or even for economic progress. It is, literally, "assistance." It is a means of helping and supplementing the efforts of nations which are able to mobilize the resources and energies of their own people. There are no shortcuts to economic and social progress.

This is a reality, but also a source of hope. For collaborative effort can achieve much. And it is increasingly understood among developed and developing nations that economic development is an international responsibility.

Many of the frustrations and disappointments of development have come not so much from the failure of programs as from the gap between results and expectations. A new understanding of the scope of the challenge and the capacity of programs will help us set feasible goals, and then achieve them.

What will be America's part in this effort?

When I came into office, it was clear that our present assistance program did not meet the realities or needs of the 1970's. It was time for a searching reassessment of our objectives and the effectiveness of our institutions. I therefore named a Task Force on International Development, chaired by Mr. Rudolph Peterson, to explore the purposes and methods of our foreign assistance. Its report, due shortly, will provide the foundation for a new American policy.

One truth is already clear: a new American purpose and attitude are required, if our economic assistance is to contribute to development in the new environment of the 1970's. As I stated on October 31 in my address on Latin America:

"For years, we in the United States have pursued the illusion that we alone could remake continents. Conscious of our wealth and technology, seized by the force of good intentions, driven by habitual impatience, remembering the dramatic success of the Marshall Plan in postwar Europe, we have sometimes imagined that we knew what was best for everyone else and that we could and should make it happen. Well, experience has taught us better.

"It has taught us that economic and social development is not an achievement of one nation's foreign policy, but something deeply rooted in each nation's own traditions.

"It has taught us that aid that infringes pride is no favor to any nation.

"It has taught us that each nation, and each region, must be true to its own character."

In our reappraisal of the purposes and techniques of foreign assistance, we have already reached several conclusions and we have adopted policies to begin to carry them out:

—*Multilateral institutions must play an increasing role in the provision of aid.* We must enlist the expertise of other countries and of international agencies, thereby minimizing the political and ideological complications which can distort the assistance relationship. We are already contributing to a number of international and regional institutions: the International Development Association, the Inter-American Development Bank, and the Asian Development Bank. I will shortly propose a new U.S. contribution to the Special Funds of the Asian Bank. And I am prepared to respond positively to proposals for replenishment of the resources of the Inter-American Bank and the International Development Association.

—*The developing countries themselves must play a larger part in formulating their own development strategies.* Their own knowledge of the needs must be applied, their own energies mobilized to the tasks. This is the approach I emphasized in my address on Latin America.

—*Our bilateral aid must carry fewer restrictions.* I have therefore eliminated some of the most onerous restrictions on the U.S. aid program and have directed that all remaining restrictions be reviewed with the objective of modifying or eliminating them.

—*Private investment must play a central role in the development process, to whatever extent desired by the developing nations themselves.* I proposed, and Congress has authorized, an Overseas Private Investment Corporation to improve our efforts to make effective use of private capital. And we have given special attention to the developing countries in our relaxation of restraints on foreign investment by U.S. corporations.

—*Trade policy must recognize the special needs of the developing countries.* Trade is a crucial source of new resources for them. Thus, as already described, I have proposed and am urging a worldwide and comprehensive system of tariff preferences for the products of developing nations.

But these are only first steps. We are already considering the proposals of the Pearson Commission on International Development, sponsored by the World Bank. When the report of the Task Force on International Development becomes available, I will propose a fresh American assistance program, more responsive to the conditions of the 1970's.

Our new foreign aid program must distinguish clearly among the various purposes our assistance is designed to serve. Grants to meet short-term emergencies need to be handled in one way, technical assistance in another, lending for long-term development in yet another. Economic development requires sustained effort by donor and recipient alike. Assistance for this purpose will be wasted if—prompted by political considerations—it is deflected by the recipient or the donor to other ends. Similarly, we shall not be putting our own resources to their most productive use if we are unable to ensure continuity in our support.

We must focus on the achievement of our real objective—effective development—rather than on some arbitrary level of financial transfer. We shall need to see that various policies affecting the development process—trade, aid, investment—are fully coordinated. And new institutions will be needed to meet the realities and the challenges of the 1970's.

Thus, our assistance program, like the rest of our foreign policy, will be changed to serve the future rather than simply continued to reflect the habits of the past. We have already begun that change. I expect a new approach to foreign assistance to be one of our major foreign policy initiatives in the coming years.

The United Nations

". . . let us press toward an open world—a world of open doors, open hearts, open minds—a world open to the exchange of ideas and of people, and open to the reach of the human spirit—a world open in the search for truth, and unconcerned with the fate of old dogmas and old isms—a world open at last to the light of justice, and the light of reason, and to the achievement of that true peace which the people of every land carry in their hearts and celebrate in their hopes."

> The President's Address to
> the 24th Session of the
> General Assembly,
> September 18, 1969

The United Nations is both a symbol of the worldwide hopes for peace and a reflection of the tensions and conflicts that have frustrated these hopes.

Its friends can now look back with pride on 25 years of accomplishment. They also have a responsibility to study and apply the lessons of those years, to see what the UN can and cannot do. The UN, and its supporters, must match idealism in purpose with realism in expectation.

Some of its accomplishments have been highly visible—particularly the various international peacekeeping efforts that have helped to damp down or control local conflicts. Other accomplishments have been quiet but no less important, and deserve greater recognition—such as its promotion of human rights and its extensive economic, social, and technical assistance programs.

The UN provides a forum for crisis diplomacy and a means for multilateral assistance. It has encouraged arms control and helped nations reach agreements extending the frontiers of international law. And it offers a framework for private discussions between world leaders, free of the inflated expectations of summit meetings.

These achievements are impressive. But we have had to recognize that the UN cannot by itself solve fundamental international disputes, especially among the superpowers. Thus, we can as easily undermine the UN by asking too much of it as too little. We cannot expect it to be a more telling force for peace than its members make it. Peace today still depends on the acts of nations.

Last September 18, in my address to the General Assembly, I said:

"In this great assembly, the desirability of peace needs no affirmation. The methods of achieving it are what so greatly challenge our courage, our intelligence, our discernment.

"And surely if one lesson above all rings resoundingly among the many shattered hopes in this world, it is that good words are not a substitute for hard deeds and noble rhetoric is no guarantee of noble results."

I then suggested some specific tasks for the near future. These included:

—securing the safety of international travelers from airplane hijackings, on which the General Assembly has already acted;
—encouraging international voluntary service, which we stress both at home and in the Peace Corps overseas;
—fostering the interrelated objectives of economic development and population control;
—protecting the planet's threatened environment, a major challenge confronting us all, and to which our own nation and people are already addressing new programs and greater energies; and
—exploring the frontiers of space, an adventure whose excitement and benefits we continue to share with other nations.

In addition, as man's uses of the oceans grow, international law must keep pace. The most pressing issue regarding the law of the sea is the need to achieve agreement on the breadth of the territorial sea, to head off the threat of escalating national claims over the ocean. We also believe it important to make parallel progress in the U.N. toward establishing an internationally agreed boundary between the Continental Shelf and the deep seabeds, and on a regime for exploration of deep seabed resources.

These are issues that transcend national differences and ideology, and should respond to effective multilateral action.

In an era when man possesses the power both to explore the heavens and desolate the earth, science and technology must be marshalled and shared in the cause of peaceful progress, whatever the political differences among nations. In numerous and varied fields—the peaceful use of atomic energy, the exploration and uses of outer space, the development of the resources of the ocean and the seabeds, the protection of our environment, the uses of satellites, the development of revolutionary transportation systems—we are working with others to channel the products of technological progress to the benefit of mankind.

My speech at the General Assembly underlined this country's continuing support for the organization. My decisions to ask Congress for funds to assist the expansion of the U.N.'s New York Headquarters and to submit to the Senate the U.N. Convention on Diplomatic Privileges and Immunities are examples of this support.

This year's 25th Anniversary of the United Nations is an occasion for more than commemoration. It is a time to acknowledge its realistic possibilities and to devise ways to expand them. It is a time to set goals for the coming years, particularly in such areas as international peacekeeping, the economic and social programs symbolized by the Second Development Decade, and the new environmental challenges posed by man's technological advances.

As the United Nations begins its second quarter century, America reaffirms its strong support for the principles and promise begun at San Francisco in 1945. Our task now—as for all U.N. members—is to help the organization in steady progress toward fulfillment of that promise.

PART III

AMERICA'S STRENGTH

Shaping Our Military Posture

America's strength is the second pillar of the structure of a durable peace.

We aim for a world in which the importance of power is reduced; where peace is secure because the principal countries wish to maintain it. But this era is not yet here. We cannot entrust our future entirely to the self-restraint of countries that have not hesitated to use their power even against their allies. With respect to national defense, any President has two principal obligations: to be certain that our military preparations do not provide an incentive for aggression, but in such a way that they do not provoke an arms race which might threaten the very security we seek to protect.

A basic review of our defense policy was essential.

In January 1969 the need for such a review was compelling. Profound changes in the world called for a fresh approach to defense policy just as they required a new approach to foreign policy. In the past, technology was relatively stable; in the contemporary world a constantly changing technology produces a new element of insecurity. Formerly, any additional strength was strategically significant; today, available power threatens to outstrip rational objectives.

We had to examine the basic premises underlying our military planning and begin shaping a military posture appropriate to the environment of the 1970's.

We launched a thorough re-examination of past concepts and programs and the alternatives we should consider for the future. The review, which is continuing, produced a reform of both national security policies and decision-making processes which was the most far-reaching in almost two decades.

For the first time, the National Security Council has

had the opportunity to review a broad and complete range of national strategies for both conventional and strategic forces. This review was undertaken in terms of security and budgetary implications five years into the future. Also for the first time, the relationship of various levels of defense spending to domestic priorities was spelled out in detail for a five-year period.

As a result of this review, our interests, our foreign policy objectives, our strategies and our defense budgets are being brought into balance—with each other and with our overall national priorities.

Four factors have a special relevance to our continuing reappraisal.

—*Military and Arms Control Issues:* First, we need to ask some fundamental questions to establish the premises for our military posture. For example:
— • In shaping our strategic nuclear posture, to what extent should we seek to maintain our security through the development of our strength? To what extent should we adopt unilateral measures of restraint? The judgment is delicate: the former course runs the risk of an arms race, the latter involves the danger of an unfavorable shift in the balance of power.
— • How would either course affect the prospects for a meaningful strategic arms limitation agreement with the Soviet Union in the years ahead?
— • What spectrum of threats can the United States responsibly deal with? Is it reasonable to seek to protect against every contingency from nuclear conflict to guerrilla wars?

—*Forward Planning*: Second, we have to plan ahead. Today's national security decisions must flow from an analysis of their implications well into the future. Many decisions on defense policies and programs will not have operational consequences for several years, in some cases for as much as a decade. Because planning mistakes may not show up for several years, deferral of hard choices is often tempting. But the ultimate penalty may be disastrous. The only responsible course is to face up to our problems and to make decisions in a long-term framework.

—*National Priorities*: Third, we have to weigh our national priorities. We will almost certainly not have the funds to finance the full range of necessary domestic programs in the years ahead if we are to maintain our commitment to non-inflationary economic growth. Defense spending is of course in a special category. It must never fall short of the minimum needed for security. If it does, the problems of domestic programs may become moot. But neither must we let defense spending grow beyond that justified by the defense of our vital interests while domestic needs go unmet.

—*Integrated Planning*: Finally, planning our national security policies and programs in given countries and regions has often been fragmented among agencies. For example, our intelligence analysts, defense planners, economists, and political analysts dealing with a given country may have been using different assumptions about our policy objectives, our expectations about the future, and even the basic facts about our policy choices. There was a need for analyses which would provide a commonly understood set of facts, evaluations and policy and program choices. These would serve as a basis for consideration by the National Security Council of what we should be doing in given countries and regions.

In summary, we asked the central doctrinal questions; we looked as much as a decade ahead; we weighed our national priorities; and we sought ways of integrating the diverse aspects of our planning. In this fashion, we have reviewed the premises of our miltary policies, discarded those that no longer serve our interests, and adopted new ones suited to the 1970's. The 1971 defense budget reflects the results of our re-examination, the transition from the old strategies and policies to the new.

The Process of Defense Planning

This Administration found a defense planning process which left vague the impact of foreign policy on our military posture and provided an inadequate role for other agencies with a major stake in military issues. And it did little to relate defense and domestic priorities.

We set out to correct these deficiencies.

Insuring Balanced Decisions

Virtually every major defense issue has complex diplomatic, political, strategic and economic implications. To insure balanced decisions, we see to it that every agency has a full opportunity to contribute. The Director of the Arms Control and Disarmament Agency participates in deliberations on defense policy decisions that affect arms control prospects. In turn, the Secretary of Defense and the Joint Chiefs of Staff participate directly in the evaluation of arms control proposals. The Departments of State and Defense review with the Bureau of the Budget and the Council of Economic Advisors economic conditions that influence the magnitude of defense spending. The Department of State examines with Defense officials issues that affect our relationships with allies.

These interagency exchanges insure that I receive all views on key national security issues. Disagreements are identified and explored, not suppressed or papered over. The full range of choices is presented.

Setting Rational Priorities

Our great wealth and productive capacity still do not enable us to pursue every worthwhile national objective with unlimited means. Choices among defense strategies and budgets have a great impact on the extent to which we can pursue other national goals.

We have no precise way of measuring whether extra dollars spent for defense are more important than extra dollars spent for other needs. But we can and have described the domestic programs that are consistent with various levels of defense expenditures. The National Security Council thus has a basis for making intelligent choices concerning the allocation of available revenue among priority federal programs. I do not believe any previous President has had the benefit of such a comprehensive picture of the interrelationships among the goals he can pursue within the limits of the federal budget.

As a result, I have decided on defense strategy and budget guidelines for the next five years that are consistent not only with our national security and the maintenance of our commitments but with our national priorities as well. This Administration is now in a position to weigh the impact of future changes in defense policies and programs on the whole fabric of government objectives.

Controlling the Defense Posture—The Defense Program Review Committee

To meet the objectives of balanced decisions and rational priorities, we made a basic addition to the National Security Council system. I directed the formation of the Defense Program Review Committee, consisting of the Assistant to the President for National Security Affairs (Chairman), the Under Secretary of State, the Deputy Secretary of Defense, the Chairman of the Joint Chiefs of Staff, the Director of the Bureau of the Budget, the Director of Central Intelligence and the Chairman of the Council of Economic Advisers. The Director of the Arms Control and Disarmament Agency, the President's Science Advisor, and the Chairman of the Atomic Energy Commission participate as appropriate.

This permanent Committee reviews major defense, fiscal, policy and program issues in terms of their strategic, diplomatic, political and economic implications and advises me and the National Security Council on its findings. For example, the Committee analyzed our options for proceeding with ballistic missile defenses on four separate occasions. This year, it will analyze our major strategic and fiscal choices over the next five years, together with the doctrinal, diplomatic and strategic implications of key weapons programs. It will do so while the defense budget for Fiscal Year 1972 is still in the earliest stages of formulation. The participation in this review by the Department of State, the Arms Control and Disarmament Agency, the Council of Economic Advisers, and other agencies insures that careful analysis and balanced evaluations will be available when the National Security Council next fall reviews our choices for 1972 and beyond.

Country and Regional Analysis and Program Budgeting

A major obstacle to the implementation of a consistent and coherent foreign policy is the multitude of U.S. agencies and programs involved in activities in any one country or region. In the past it has been difficult for the President or the National Security Council to obtain a picture of the totality of our effort in any one country. Yet a rational foreign policy must start with such a comprehensive view.

To overcome this difficulty we have begun a series of country program analyses which will examine all U.S. programs in key countries and regions and their interrelationships.

The studies for the first time put every U.S. program into one budget framework. The basic tool for this analysis is the program budget, which allocates all of our expenditures in a country on the basis of the purposes served. It permits us to make decisions or set guidelines for all of our programs simultaneously; in the past, they were examined largely agency by agency in isolation from one another.

The results of the country analysis studies are presented to the NSC in the form of integrated policy and program options based on alternative statements of interests, threats, and U.S. foreign policy objectives. After the NSC has considered these options, a decision can be made about the course of action to follow over the next several years.

Of course, our efforts start from the clearly understood, fundamental premise that U.S. policies and programs must relate in a logical and meaningful fashion to what our friends and allies wish to do for themselves. We are dealing with sovereign nations each of which has its own interests, its own priorities and its own capabilities. All our country programming is designed to do is to make our actions as effective as they can be consistent with our mutual interests.

I am convinced that such a comprehensive approach to country programs will lead to a decidedly improved foreign policy. We are conscious of the need not only to make sound policy decisions but also to execute them. The country analysis studies will result in both a decision document for all government agencies and firm five-year program guidelines, presented in the form of a program budget. The members of the NSC, as well as the country director in every agency and our ambassadors in the field, then have a means of making sure that our decisions are followed up.

Strategic Policy

The Changing Strategic Balance

Following World War II, the U.S. had a monopoly of strategic nuclear weapons. Throughout most of the 1950's, our virtual monopoly of intercontinental nuclear delivery capability, in the form of a large force of Strategic Air Command bombers, gave us an overwhelming deterrent.

This assessment was unchallenged until it became apparent in the late 1950's that the Soviet Union possessed the potential for developing and deploying a force of intercontinental ballistic missiles that could destroy a large part of our strategic bomber force on the ground. The fear that our deterrent to nuclear war was in grave jeopardy, though it later proved exaggerated, focused our attention on maintaining our nuclear superiority.

In 1961, the new Administration accelerated our Polaris submarine and Minuteman ICBM programs and put more of our strategic bombers on alert. These measures provided a clear margin of U.S. nuclear superiority for several years. They restored our confidence in our deterrent; we now had two forces, our Polaris submarines and our Minuteman ICBM's, deployed in hardened underground silos, that were virtually invulnerable to attack by the Soviet Union with the then-existing technology.

However, after 1965, the Soviets stepped up their

ICBM deployments and began to construct their own force of Polaris-type submarines. And they began to test multiple warheads for their SS-9 ICBM, a weapon which can carry roughly ten times as much as our Minuteman missile.

Once again, U.S. strategic superiority was being challenged. However, this time, the Johnson Administration decided not to step up deployments. This restraint was based on two judgments. First, it was believed that there was relatively little we could do to keep the Soviets from developing over a period of time a strategic posture comparable in capability to our own. Second, it was thought that nuclear superiority of the kind we had previously enjoyed would have little military or political significance because our retaliatory capability was not seriously jeopardized by larger Soviet forces and because their goal was in all likelihood a retaliatory capability similar to ours.

As a result of these developments, an inescapable reality of the 1970's is the Soviet Union's possession of powerful and sophisticated strategic forces approaching, and in some categories, exceeding ours in numbers and capability.

Recent Soviet programs have emphasized both quantitative increases in offensive and defensive forces and qualitative improvements in the capabilities of these forces —such as a new, more accurate warhead and perhaps penetration aids for their Minuteman-type SS-11 missile, continued testing of the multiple warhead for the SS-9, and research and development on improved components for their ABM system, together with improved coverage by their ABM radars. The following table shows the growth in Soviet land- and submarine-based missile forces in the last five years.

OPERATIONAL U.S. AND SOVIET MISSILES

	1965 (Mid-Year)	1970 (Projected) (For Year End)
Intercontinental Ballistic Missiles		
U.S.	934	1,054
Soviet	224	1,290
Submarine Launched Ballistic Missiles		
U.S.	464	656
Soviet	107	300

The Soviet missile deployments are continuing, whereas ours have leveled off. In the 1970's we must also expect to see Communist China deploy intercontinental ballistic missiles, seriously complicating strategic planning and diplomacy.

The evolution of U.S. and Soviet strategic capabilities during the past two decades was accompanied by intense doctrinal debates over the political and military roles of strategic forces and the appropriate criteria for choosing them.

The strategic doctrine that had gained the greatest acceptance by the time my Administration took office was this: According to the theory of "assured destruction," deterrence was guaranteed if we were sure we could destroy a significant percentage of Soviet population and industry after the worst conceivable Soviet attack on our strategic forces. The previous Administration reasoned that since we had more than enough forces for this purpose, restraint in the build-up of strategic weapons was indicated regardless of Soviet actions. Further, it hoped that U.S. restraint in strategic weapons developments and deployments would provide a strong incentive for similar restraint by the Soviet Union, thus enhancing the likelihood of a stable strategic relationship between the two nuclear superpowers.

A Policy for the 1970's

Once in office, I concluded that this strategic doctrine should be carefully reviewed in the light of the continued growth of Soviet strategic capabilities. Since the Soviets were continuing their ambitious strategic weapons program, we had to ask some basic questions. Why might a nuclear war start or be threatened? In this light, what U.S. strategic capabilities are needed for deterrence?

We sought, in short, a strategic goal that can best be termed "sufficiency."

Our review took full account of two factors that have not existed in the past.

First, the Soviets' present build-up of strategic forces, together with what we know about their development and test programs, raises serious questions about where they are headed and the potential threats we and our allies face. These questions must be faced soberly and realistically.

Second, the growing strategic forces on both sides pose new and disturbing problems. Should a President, in the event of a nuclear attack, be left with the single option of ordering the mass destruction of enemy civilians, in the face of the certainty that it would be followed by the mass slaughter of Americans? Should the concept of assured destruction be narrowly defined and should it be the only measure of our ability to deter the variety of threats we may face?

Our review produced general agreement that the overriding purpose of our strategic posture is political and defensive: to deny other countries the ability to impose their will on the United States and its allies under the weight of strategic military superiority. We must insure that all potential aggressors see unacceptable risks in contemplating a nuclear attack, or nuclear blackmail, or acts which could escalate to strategic nuclear war, such as a Soviet conventional attack on Europe.

Beyond this general statement, our primary task was to decide on the yardstick that should be used in evaluating the adequacy of our strategic forces against the projected threats. This issue took on added importance because such yardsticks would be needed for assessing the desirability of possible strategic arms limitation agreements with the Soviet Union.

We reached general agreement within the government on four specific criteria for strategic sufficiency. These represent a significant intellectual advance. They provide for both adequacy and flexibility. They will be constantly reviewed in the light of a changing technology.

Designing Strategic Forces

Having settled on a statement of strategic purposes and criteria, we analyzed possible U.S. strategic force postures for the 1970's and beyond. We reviewed alternatives ranging from "minimum deterrence"—a posture built around ballistic missile submarines and the assured destruction doctrine narrowly interpreted—to attempts at recapturing numerical superiority through accelerated U.S. strategic deployments across the board.

There was general agreement that postures which significantly reduced or increased our strategic programs and deployments involved undesirable risks:

—*Sharp cutbacks would not permit us to satisfy our sufficiency criteria, and might provoke the opposite Soviet reaction.* If the U.S. unilaterally dropped out of the strategic arms competition, the Soviets might well seize the opportunity to step up their programs and achieve a significant margin of strategic superiority. The vigor and breadth of their current strategic weapons programs and deployments, which clearly exceed the requirements of minimum deterrence, make such a possibility seem far from remote. They might also—paradoxically—eliminate any Soviet incentives for an agreement to limit strategic arms, and would raise serious concerns among our allies. This is particularly true for our NATO allies who view the U.S. commitment to deter Soviet aggression as being based mainly on our maintenance of a powerful strategic posture.

—*Sharp increases, on the other hand, might not have any significant political or military benefits.* Many believe that the Soviets would seek to offset our actions, at least in part, and that Soviet political positions would harden, tensions would increase, and the prospect for reaching agreements to limit strategic arms might be irreparably damaged.

What ultimately we must do in between these extremes will depend, of course, on many factors. Will the Soviets continue to expand their strategic forces? What will be their configuration? What understanding might we reach on strategic arms limitations? What weapons systems might be covered by agreements?

I recognize that decisions on shaping our strategic posture are perhaps the most complex and fateful we face. The answers to these questions will largely determine whether we will be forced into increased deployments to offset the Soviet threat to the sufficiency of our deterrent, or whether we and the Soviet Union can together move from an era of confrontation to one of negotiation, whether jointly we can pursue responsible, non-provocative strategic arms policies based on sufficiency as a mutually shared goal or whether there will be another round of the arms race.

The Role of Ballistic Missile Defense

My decision to continue with the construction of the Safeguard anti-ballistic missile system is fully consistent with our criteria and with our goal of effective arms limitation.

I would like to recall what I said last March about the problem that led us to seek approval of the first phase of the Safeguard program:

> "The gravest responsibility which I bear as President of the United States is for the security of the Nation. Our nuclear forces defend not only ourselves but our allies as well. The imperative that our nuclear deterrent remain secure beyond any possible doubt requires that the U.S. must take steps now to insure that our strategic retaliatory forces will not become vulnerable to a Soviet attack."

I believed then, and I am even more convinced today, that there is a serious threat to our retaliatory capability in the form of the growing Soviet forces of ICBM's and ballistic missile submarines, their multiple warhead program for the SS-9 missile, their apparent interest in improving the accuracy of their ICBM warheads, and their development of a semi-orbital nuclear weapon system. That this threat continues to be serious was confirmed by my Foreign Intelligence Advisory Board—an independent, bipartisan group of senior outside advisors—which recently completed its own review of the strategic threats we face.

I pointed out in the same statement that we cannot ignore the potential Chinese threat against the U.S. population, as well as the danger of an accidental or unauthorized attack from any source. Nor can we dismiss the possibility that other countries may in the future acquire the capability to attack the U.S. with nuclear weapons. Today, any nuclear attack—no matter how small; whether accidental, unauthorized or by design; by a superpower or a country with only a primitive nuclear delivery capability—would be a catastophe for the U.S., no matter how devastating our ability to retaliate.

No Administration with the responsibility for the lives and security of the American people could fail to provide every possible protection against such eventualities.

Thus on March 14, 1969, I stated the objectives of the Safeguard program:

"This measured deployment is designed to fulfill three objectives:
"1. Protection of our land-based retaliatory forces against a direct attack by the Soviet Union.
"2. Defense of the American people against the kind of nuclear attack which Communist China is likely to be able to mount within the decade.
"3. Protection againt the possibility of accidental attacks."

I further described the system as follows:

"We will provide for local defense of selected Minuteman missile sites and an area defense designed to protect our bomber bases and our command and control authorities. In addition, this system will provide a defense of the Continental United States against an accidental attack and will provide substantial protection against the kind of attack which the Chinese Communists may be capable of launching throughout the 1970's. This deployment will not require us to place missile and radar sites close to our major cities."

Last year, I promised that "each phase of the deployment will be reviewed to insure that we are doing as much as necessary but not more than that required by the threat existing at that time." I further indicated that in strategic arms limitation talks with the Soviet Unon, the United States will be fully prepared to discuss limitations on defensive as well as offensive weapons systems.

The further steps I shall propose will be consistent with these pledges. The Secretary of Defense will put forward a minimum program essential for our security. It fully protects our flexibility in discussing limitations on defensive weapons with the Soviet Union. It is my duty as President to make certain that we do no less.

General Purpose Forces

Premises

When I examined the objectives established for our general purpose forces, I concluded that we must emphasize three fundamental premises of a sound defense policy:

First, while strategic forces must deter *all* threats of general war no matter what the cost, our general purpose forces must be more sensitively related to local situations and particular interests.

Second, while the possession of 95 per cent of the nuclear power of the non-Communist world gives us the primary responsibility for nuclear defense, the planning of general purpose forces must take into account the fact that the manpower of our friends greatly exceeds our own, as well as our heavy expenditures for strategic forces.

Third, we cannot expect U.S. military forces to cope with the entire spectrum of threats facing allies or potential allies throughout the world. This is particularly true of subversion and guerrilla warfare, or "wars of national liberation." Experience has shown that the best means of dealing with insurgencies is to preempt them through economic development and social reform and to control them with police, paramilitary and military action by the threatened government.

We may be able to supplement local efforts with economic and military assistance. However, a direct combat role for U.S. general purpose forces arises primarily when insurgency has shaded into external aggression or when there is an overt conventional attack. In such cases, we shall weigh our interests and our commitments, and we shall consider the efforts of our allies, in determining our response.

The United States has interests in defending certain land areas abroad as well as essential air and sea lines of communication. These derive from:

—the political and economic importance of our alliances;
—our desire to prevent or contain hostilities which could lead to major conflicts and thereby endanger world peace; and
—the strategic value of the threatened area as well as its line of communications.

The military posture review I initiated the day I took office included a thorough examination of our general purpose forces. This study explored in turn our interests, the potential threats to those interests, the capabilities of our allies both with and without our assistance, and the relationship of various strategies to domestic priorities.

The National Security Council examined five different strategies for general purpose forces and related each one to the domestic programs which could be supported simultaneously. Thus, for the first time, national security and domestic priorities were considered together. In fact, two strategies were rejected because they were not considered essential to our security and because they would have thwarted vital domestic programs.

We finally decided on a strategy which represented a significant modification of the doctrine that characterized the 1960's.

The stated basis of our conventional posture in the 1960's was the so-called "2-½ war" principle. According to it, U.S. forces would be maintained for a three-month conventional forward defense of NATO, a defense of Korea or Southeast Asia against a full-scale Chinese attack, and a minor contingency—all simultaneously. These force levels were never reached.

In the effort to harmonize doctrine and capability, we chose what is best described as the "1-½ war" strategy. Under it we will maintain in peacetime general purpose forces adequate for simultaneously meeting a major Communist attack in either Europe or Asia, assisting allies against non-Chinese threats in Asia, and contending with a contingency elsewhere.

The choice of this strategy was based on the following considerations:

—the nuclear capability of our strategic and theater nuclear forces serves as a deterrent to full-scale Soviet attack on NATO Europe or Chinese attack on our Asian allies;

—the prospects for a coordinated two-front attack on our allies by Russia and China are low both because of the risks of nuclear war and the improbability of Sino-Soviet cooperation. In any event, we do not believe that such a coordinated attack should be met primarily by U.S. conventional forces;

—the desirability of insuring against greater than expected threats by maintaining more than the forces required to meet conventional threats in one theater—such as NATO Europe;

—weakness on our part would be more provocative than continued U.S. strength, for it might encourage others to take dangerous risks, to resort to the illusion that military adventurism could succeed.

To meet the requirements for the strategy we adopted, we will maintain the required ground and supporting tactical air forces in Europe and Asia, together with naval and air forces. At the same time, we will retain adequate active forces in addition to a full complement of reserve forces based in the United States. These force levels will be spelled out in greater detail in the program and budget statement of the Secretary of Defense.

PART IV

AN ERA OF NEGOTIATION

> "We cannot expect to make every one our friend but we can try to make no one our enemy."
> The President's Inaugural Address

Twenty years ago the United States and what was then the Communist bloc could be resigned to the mutual hostility that flowed from deep-seated differences of ideology and national purpose. Many of those differences remain today. But the changes of two decades have brought new conditions and magnified the risks of intractable hostility.

—For us as well as our adversaries, in the nuclear age the perils of using force are simply not in reasonable proportion to most of the objectives sought in many cases. The balance of nuclear power has placed a premium on negotiation rather than confrontation.
—We both have learned too that great powers may find their interests deeply involved in local conflict—risking confrontation—yet have precariously little influence over the direction taken by local forces.
—The nuclear age has also posed for the United States and the Communist countries the common dangers of accident or miscalculation. Both sides are threatened, for example, when any power seeks tactical advantage from a crisis and risks provoking a strategic response.
—Reality has proved different from expectation for both sides. The Communist world in particular has had to learn that the spread of Communism may magnify international tensions rather than usher in a period of reconciliation as Marx taught.

Thus, in a changing world, building peace requires patient and continuing communication. Our first task in that dialogue is fundamental—to avert war. Beyond that, the United States and the Communist countries must negotiate on the issues that divide them if we are to build a durable peace. Since these issues were not caused by personal disagreements, they cannot be removed by mere atmospherics. We do not delude ourselves that a change of tone represents a change of policy. We are prepared to deal seriously, concretely and precisely with outstanding issues.

The lessons of the post-war period in negotiations with the Communist states—a record of some success, though much more of frustration—point to three clear principles which this Administration will observe in approaching negotiations in the 1970's.

First: We will deal with the Communist countries on the basis of a precise understanding of what they are about in the world, and thus of what we can reasonably expect of them and ourselves. Let us make no mistake about it—leaders of the Communist nations are serious and determined. Because we do take them seriously, we will not underestimate the depth of ideological disagreement or the disparity between their interests and ours. Nor will we pretend that agreement is imminent by fostering the illusion that they have already given up their beliefs or are just about to do so in the process of negotiations.

It is precisely these differences which require creation of objective conditions—negotiation by negotiation—from which peace can develop despite a history of mistrust and rivalry. We may hope that the passage of time and the emergence of a new generation in the Communist countries will bring some change in Communist purposes. But failing that, we must seek in the most practical way to influence Communist actions.

It will be the policy of the United States, therefore, not to employ negotiations as a forum for cold-war invective, or ideological debate. We will regard our Communist adversaries first and foremost as nations pursuing their own interests as *they* perceive these interests, just as we follow our own interests as we see them. We will judge them by their actions as we expect to be judged by our own. Specific agreements, and the structure of peace they help build, will come from a realistic accommodation of conflicting interests.

A second principle we shall observe in negotiating with the Communist countries relates to how these negotiations should be conducted—how they should be judged by peoples on both sides anxious for an easing of tensions. All too often in the past, whether at the summit or lower levels, we have come to the conference table with more attention to psychological effect than to substance. Naive enthusiasm and even exaltation about the fact that a negotiation will be held only tends to obscure the real issues on whose resolution the success of the talks depends. Then, since the results are almost always less dramatic than expected, the false euphoria gives way to equally false hopelessness.

Negotiations must be, above all, the result of careful preparation and an authentic give-and-take on the issues which have given rise to them. They are served by neither bluff abroad nor bluster at home.

We will not become psychologically dependent on rapid or extravagant progress. Nor will we be discouraged by frustration or seeming failure. The stakes are too high, and the task too great, to judge our effort in any temporary perspective. We shall match our purpose with perseverance.

The third essential in successful negotiations is an appreciation of the context in which issues are addressed. The central fact here is the inter-relationship of international events. We did not invent the inter-relationship; it is not a negotiating tactic. It is a fact of life. This Administration recognizes that international developments are entwined in many complex ways: political issues relate to strategic questions, political events in one area of the world may have a far-reaching effect on political developments in other parts of the globe.

These principles emphasize a realistic approach to seeking peace through negotiations. They are a guide to a gradual and practical process of building agreement on agreement. They rest upon the basic reality which underlies this Administration's dealings with the Communist states. We will not trade principles for promises, or vital interests for atmosphere. We shall always be ready to talk seriously and purposefully about the building of a stable peace.

The Soviet Union

The general principles outlined above apply fully to our approach to issues between the United States and the Soviet Union.

The Soviet Union shares with other countries the overwhelming temptation to continue to base its policies at home and abroad on old and familiar concepts. But perceptions framed in the Nineteenth Century are hardly relevant to the new era we are now entering.

If we have had to learn the limitations of our own power, the lessons of the last two decades must have left their imprint on the leadership in the Kremlin—in the recognition that Marxist ideology is not the surest guide to the problems of a changing industrial society, the worldwide decline in the appeal of ideology, and most of all in the foreign policy dilemmas repeatedly posed by the spread of Communism to states which refuse to endure permanent submission to Soviet authority—a development illustrated vividly by the Soviet schism with China.

The central problem of Soviet-American relations, then, is whether our two countries can transcend the past and work together to build a lasting peace.

In 1969, we made a good beginning. In this first year of my Administration we ratified the Non-Proliferation Treaty; we made progress in negotiating arms control on the seabed; we took steps to further the prospects of agreement regarding chemical and biological methods of warfare; we engaged in talks on a Middle Eastern settlement; and we began negotiations on the limitation of strategic arms—the most important arms control negotiations this country has ever entered. In concert with our allies, we have also offered to negotiate on specific issues in Europe: history has taught us that if crises arise in Europe, the world at large cannot long expect to remain unaffected.

But while certain successes have been registered in negotiations and there is cause for cautious optimism that others will follow, our overall relationship with the USSR remains far from satisfactory. To the detriment of the cause of peace, the Soviet leadership has failed to exert a helpful influence on the North Vietnamese in Paris. The overwhelming majority of the war materiel that reaches North Vietnam comes from the USSR, which thereby bears a heavy responsibility for the continuation of the war. This cannot help but cloud the rest of our relationship with the Soviet Union.

In the Middle East talks, too, we have not seen on the Soviet side that practical and constructive flexibility which is necessary for a successful outcome, and without which the responsibility of the great powers in the search for a settlement cannot be met. We see evidence, moreover, that the Soviet Union seeks a position in the area as a whole which would make great power rivalry more likely.

We hope that the coming year will bring evidence that the Soviets have decided to seek a durable peace rather than continue along the roads of the past.

It will not be the sincerity or purpose of the Soviet leadership that will be at issue. The tensions between us are not generated by personal misunderstandings, and neither side does anyone a service by so suggesting. Peace does not come simply with statesmen's smiles. At issue are basic questions of long conflicting purposes in a world where no one's interests are furthered by conflict. Only a straightforward recognition of that reality—and an equally direct effort to deal with it—will bring us to the genuine cooperation which we seek and which the peace of the world requires.

Eastern Europe

The nations of Eastern Europe have a history with many tragic aspects. Astride the traditional invasion routes of the Continent, they have suffered long periods of foreign occupation and cultural suppression. And even when they gained independence—many of them following World War I—they remained the prey of powerful neighbors.

We are aware that the Soviet Union sees its own security as directly affected by developments in this region.

Several times, over the centuries, Russia has been invaded through Central Europe; so this sensitivity is not novel, or purely the product of Communist dogma.

It is not the intention of the United States to undermine the legitimate security interests of the Soviet Union. The time is certainly past, with the development of modern technology, when any power would seek to exploit Eastern Europe to obtain strategic advantage against the Soviet Union. It is clearly no part of our policy. Our pursuit of negotiation and detente is meant to reduce existing tensions, not to stir up new ones.

By the same token, the United States views the countries of Eastern Europe as sovereign, not as parts of a monolith. And we can accept no doctrine that abridges their right to seek reciprocal improvement of relations with us or others.

We are prepared to enter into negotiations with the nations of Eastern Europe, looking to a gradual normalization of relations. We will adjust ourselves to whatever pace and extent of normalization these countries are willing to sustain.

Progress in this direction has already been achieved in our relations with Romania. My visit to that country last summer—which will remain unforgettable for me in human terms—set in motion a series of cooperative programs in the economic, technical, scientific and cultural fields. We intend to pursue these with vigor. My talks with President Ceausescu also began the process of exchanging views on broader questions of mutual concern which, in our view, will contribute to a general improvement of the communication between West and East. A similar relationship is open to any Communist country that wishes to enter it.

Stability and peace in Europe will be enhanced once its division is healed. The United States, and the nations of Western Europe, have historic ties with the peoples and nations of Eastern Europe, which we wish to maintain and renew.

As I said in my toast to President Ceausescu during my visit to Romania last August:

"We seek, in sum, a peace not of hegemonies, and not of artificial uniformity, but a peace in which the legitimate interests of each are respected and all are safeguarded."

Communist China

The Chinese are a great and vital people who should not remain isolated from the international community. In the long run, no stable and enduring international order is conceivable without the contribution of this nation of more than 700 million people.

Chinese foreign policy reflects the complexity of China's historical relationships with the outside world. While China has the longest unbroken history of self-government in the world, it has had little experience in dealing with other nations on a basis of equal sovereignty. Predominant in Asia for many centuries, these gifted and cultured people saw their society as the center of the world. Their tradition of self-imposed cultural isolation ended abruptly in the Nineteenth Century, however, when an internally weak China fell prey to exploitation by technologically superior foreign powers.

The history inherited by the Chinese Communists, therefore, was a complicated mixture of isolation and incursion, of pride and humiliation. We must recall this unique past when we attempt to define a new relationship for the future.

Nor can we underestimate the gulf of ideology between us, or the apparent differences in interests and how we interpret world events. While America has historic ties of friendship with the Chinese people, and many of our basic interests are not in conflict, we must recognize the profound gulf of suspicion and ideology.

The principles underlying our relations with Communist China are similar to those governing our policies toward the USSR. United States policy is not likely soon to have much impact on China's behavior, let alone its ideological outlook. But it is certainly in our interest, and in the interest of peace and stability in Asia and the world, that we take what steps we can toward improved practical relations with Peking.

The key to our relations will be the actions each side takes regarding the other and its allies. We will not ignore hostile acts. We intend to maintain our treaty commitment to the defense of the Republic of China. But we will seek to promote understandings which can establish a new pattern of mutually beneficial actions.

I made these points to the leaders I met throughout my trip to Asia, and they were welcomed as constructive and realistic.

We have avoided dramatic gestures which might invite dramatic rebuffs. We have taken specific steps that did not require Chinese agreement but which underlined our willingness to have a more normal and constructive relationship. During the year, we have:

—made it possible for American tourists, museums, and others to make non-commercial purchases of Chinese goods without special authorization;
—broadened the categories of Americans whose passports may be automatically validated for travel in Communist China, to include members of Congress, journalists, teachers, post-graduate scholars and college students, scientists, medical doctors and representatives of the American Red Cross;
—permitted subsidiaries of American firms abroad to engage in commerce between Communist China and third countries.

The resumption of talks with the Chinese in Warsaw may indicate that our approach will prove useful. These first steps may not lead to major results at once, but sooner or later Communist China will be ready to re-enter the international community.

Our desire for improved relations is not a tactical means of exploiting the clash between China and the Soviet Union. We see no benefit to us in the intensification of that conflict, and we have no intention of taking sides. Nor is the United States interested in joining any condominium or hostile coalition of great powers against either of the large Communist countries. Our attitude is clearcut—a lasting peace will be impossible so long as some nations consider themselves the permanent enemies of others.

Arms Control

There is no area in which we and the Soviet Union—as well as others—have a greater common interest than in reaching agreement with regard to arms control.

The traditional course of seeking security primarily through military strength raises several problems in a world of multiplying strategic weapons.

—Modern technology makes any balance precarious and prompts new efforts at ever higher levels of complexity.
—Such an arms race absorbs resources, talents and energies.
—The more intense the competition, the greater the uncertainty about the other side's intentions.
—The high the level of armaments, the greater the violence and devastation should deterrence fail.

For these reasons I decided early in the Administration that we should seek to maintain our security whenever possible through cooperative efforts with other nations at the lowest possible level of uncertainty, cost, and potential violence.

Our careful preparations for the Strategic Arms Limitation Talks (SALT) with the Soviet Union were designed to achieve this objective.

Preparations for SALT

Our immediate problem was to determine what measures would be most practical in slowing the momentum of armament and work out a procedure most likely to yield useful discussions.

In preparing for these negotiations, we were tempted to follow the traditional pattern of settling on one agreed position and launching discussions with the other side on this basis. We could have adopted the specific package proposal developed by the previous Administration or we could have quickly formulated an alternative plan. In my judgment there were two major problems with this approach.

First, I was convinced that we lacked the comprehensive and detailed body of facts and analyses to take account of the most recent developments in Soviet and U.S. strategic programs.

Second, we would have been engaged in a negotiating process—with the inevitable investment of prestige—before either side had defined its purposes. There was a danger of turning SALT into a tactical exercise or even more the kind of propaganda battle characteristic of some previous disarmament conferences.

Too much depended on these talks, for our nation and all mankind, to rush into them partially prepared. We decided that a clarification of objectives and factual data would allow us to discuss proposals in a coherent framework, and ultimately speed up negotiations. We assumed further that if the other side had a serious interest in exploring the possibilities of strategic arms limitations they would have a joint interest with us to analyze the issues which would have to be resolved before a satisfactory agreement could be reached. For an agreement to limit strategic arms can be lasting only if it enhances the sense of security of *both* sides. It is in the mutual interest therefore to clarify each other's intentions.

Therefore, instead of attempting to hammer out an agreed government position or a simple proposal, we chose a different course.

We first laid out preliminary models of possible strategic arms limitation agreements. We compared these both with each other and with the situation most likely to prevail in the absence of an agreement. This process greatly improved our understanding of the types of agreements we should consider and pointed up some of the fundamental issues. In order to resolve these issues, I directed the formation of a Verification Panel to examine the verification aspects and strategic implications of curbs on individual weapons systems and then combinations of them.

The Panel took each strategic weapons system in isolation (e.g., ICBM's or ABM's) and explored all the issues that would be involved in its limitation. We knew that any agreement had to be verified and we knew too the reluctance of the Soviet Union to accept on-site inspection. The Verification Panel therefore analyzed in detail what we could do unilaterally. Specifically, it surveyed our intelligence capability to monitor the other side's compliance with a curb for each weapon system; the precise activities that would have to be restricted to ensure confidence in the effectiveness of the limitation; and the impact of the limitation on U.S. and Soviet strategic weapons programs.

The analysis of our capability to verify individual weapons systems provided the building blocks for analyzing various combinations of limitations. These building blocks were combined in various positions which can be grouped in three general categories. This will enable us to respond to a broad range of Soviet proposals. These categories are:

1. *Limitations on numbers of missiles.* A ceiling would be placed on numbers of missiles without an attempt to restrain qualitative improvements like MIRV (multiple independently targeted re-entry vehicles). In general, these options would stop the growth of some or all strategic missile forces. They would not change the qualitative race.

2. *Limitations on numbers and capabilities of missiles.* These options would not only limit the numbers of missiles but also their capabilities, including qualitative controls over such weapons as MIRV's. The hard issues here center around verification since the determination of quality requires a more intensive inspection than quantity.

3. *Reduce offensive forces.* This approach would attempt to reduce the number of offensive forces without qualitative restrictions on the theory that at fixed and lower levels of armaments the risks of technological surprise would be reduced.

Each of these options was analyzed in relation to various levels of strategic defensive missiles, ABM's.

The manner in which these studies were carried out

contributed to their scope and their success. Discussions explored substantive issues rather than exchanging rigidly defined bureaucratic positions. Consistent with the overall philosophy of the NSC system, we focused on comprehensive assessments of the issues and alternatives rather than on attainable compromises. This presented me with clear choices, clear disagreements, and clear rationales. In the process we established a comprehensive inventory of the possibilities of a wide range of limitations. This should greatly enhance our flexibility in the forthcoming negotiations.

The SALT negotiations involve fundamental security issues for our NATO allies, as well as Japan. We have fully consulted them, engaging their views and expertise at every stage of the process. In July we discussed in great detail the relationship of SALT to the overall strategic balance with our allies and we presented the various options as we saw them then. In early November we consulted in greater detail on our approach to the first phase of SALT. We intend to continue to work closely with our allies as the negotiations continue. We consider our security inseparable from theirs.

This process involved the most intensive study of strategic arms problems ever made by this or any other government. And this process had several advantages. We were not tied to a single position; instead we had building blocks for several different positions depending on our decisions and what might prove negotiable. Opening talks with the Soviets could concentrate on the principles and objectives underlying *any* type of strategic arms agreement.

Preliminary talks in Helsinki opened November 17 and continued until December 22. Our experience there confirmed the validity of our approach. The discussions were serious and businesslike. The Soviet representatives demonstrated considerable preparation. They also seemed to welcome the "building block" approach. We were able to develop an agreed work program for further discussions without acrimony and in full awareness of the likely nature of such discussions. Above all, we could explore each other's purposes without getting bogged down in negotiating details.

From a discussion of basic principles and objectives we plan to move in April in Vienna to more specific positions. We enter this next phase with a well-developed body of technical analysis and evaluations, which is being continuously expanded and improved by the Verification Panel and the NSC process. And we will make a determined effort throughout these negotiations to reach agreements that will not only protect our national security but actually enhance it.

Chemical and Biological Weapons

We are prepared to take any unilateral arms control action that will not compromise our security and will minimize the danger that certain weapons will ever be developed or used by any nation. A good example is the field of chemical and biological weapons. After extensive study, I determined that a new American policy would strengthen ongoing multilateral efforts to restrict the use of these weapons by international law. We hope that other nations will follow our example and restrict their own programs unilaterally.

When I took office, the chemical and biological defense programs of the United States had gone unexamined and unanalyzed by policymakers for 15 years. I directed a comprehensive NSC system review of the premises, issues, and technical details involved. This major six-month study was the first thorough reassessment of this subject that had ever taken place at the Presidential level. After a National Security Council meeting in early November, I announced my specific decisions on November 25:

—*Chemical Warfare:* First, I reaffirmed the long-standing policy that the United States will never be the first to use lethal chemicals in any conflict. Second, I extended this policy to include incapacitating chemical weapons. Third, I am submitting the 1925 Geneva Protocol—which prohibits the use of chemical and biological weapons in warfare—to the Senate for its advice and consent to ratification.

—*Biological Research:* I declared that the United States is renouncing biological warfare, since biological warfare would have massive, unpredictable, and potentially uncontrollable consequences. The United States will not engage in the development, procurement, or stockpiling of biological weapons. We shall restrict our biological program to research for defensive purposes, strictly defined—such as techniques of immunization, safety measures, and the control and prevention of the spread of disease. The United States has associated itself with the objectives of the United Kingdom draft convention banning the use of biological weapons, submitted to the Conference of the Committee on Disarmament at Geneva in 1969.

In addition, on February 14, 1970, the United States renounced offensive preparations for the use of toxins as a method of warfare. We declared that we will confine our military programs for toxins to research for defensive purposes only, and announced that all existing toxin weapons and stocks of toxins which are not required for this research would be destroyed. Although the U.N. Secretary General and World Health Organization have declared that toxins are chemicals, they produce effects commonly described as disease, and are produced by facilities similar to those needed for the production of biological agents. Hence we decided to remove any ambiguity in the interest of progress toward arms control.

As I stated on November 25, "Mankind already carries in its own hands too many of the seeds of its own destruction." By the examples we set, we hope to lead the way toward the day when other nations adopt the same principles.

Seabeds—Multilateral Arms Control

The responsibility for the control of armaments is multilateral as well as bilateral. The spread of technological skills knows no national boundaries; and innovation in weaponry is no monopoly of the superpowers. The danger of competitive armament is universal. Without international constraints, the planet would be menaced by the spread of weapons of mass destruction to regions newly explored.

Collaborative efforts to avert these dangers have already produced a series of international agreements:

—to prohibit the testing of nuclear weapons in the atmosphere, in outer space, and underwater.
—to prohibit the proliferation of nuclear weaponry.
—to prohibit the use of Antarctica, or of outer space and its celestial bodies, for military purposes.

The United States has supported the efforts of the Conference of the Committee on Disarmament at Geneva to reach an international agreement prohibiting the emplacement of weapons of mass destruction on the bed of the sea. It is to the advantage of all to bring arms control, instead of strategic arms, to the ocean floor. The spread of weapons of mass destruction to this new realm would complicate the security problem of all nations, and would be to no nation's advantage.

Conclusion

The first year of this Administration saw significant progress in three areas of arms control.

—Unilaterally, we announced the comprehensive chemical and biological policy designed to set an example and encourage multilateral arms control in this field.
—Bilaterally, with the Soviet Union, we launched what could be the most important arms control discussions ever undertaken.
—Multilaterally, we made substantial progress toward reserving the vast ocean floors for peaceful purposes.

In all three instances we see our actions as protecting America's strength and enhancing her security. It is the biggest responsibility of this generation to avoid becoming the victim of its own technology.

Issues for the Future

The issues before us are ample proof of the challenge we face. The agenda requires not only fateful re-examinations of some of our old positions but also judgments about trends in the Communist world and the effect of our negotiations on our relationship with our friends. These questions include:

1. STRATEGIC ARMS LIMITATIONS Our approach to these negotiations has been described in detail above.
2. LIMITING THE FLOW OF WEAPONS TO REGIONS IN CONFLICT When peace is in everyone's interest, we must find a way to control conflict everywhere. We must not be drawn into conflicts by local rivalries. The great powers should try to damp down rather than fan local passions by showing restraint in their sale of arms to regions in conflict. We stand ready to discuss practical arrangements to this end.
3. RESOLVE THE GREAT EAST-WEST POLITICAL ISSUES We continue to be prepared to discuss the issues that divide us from the Communist countries. Whether in addressing the cruel division of Europe or the future security of Asia we shall try to deepen the dialogue with the Communist powers. But we will not permit negotiations to be used to sacrifice the interests of our friends. We are committed to the closest consultation with our NATO allies, and we will maintain the closest contact with our friends and allies in Asia.
4. CLOSER COOPERATION IN POTENTIAL CRISES We must give practical expression to the common interest we have with the Soviet Union in identifying or limiting conflict in various areas of the world. Our choice is to find a way to share more information with our adversaries to head off conflict *without* affecting either our own security interests or those of our friends.

These are all difficult choices. Our careful consideration of the issues involved in negotiations with the Communist world will take full account of them, as we proceed to build a lasting peace without sacrificing the interests of our allies and friends.

CONCLUSION

A New Definition of Peace

Few ideas have been so often or so loosely invoked as that of "Peace." But if peace is among the most overworked and often-abused staples of mankind's vocabulary, one of the reasons is that it is embedded so deeply in man's aspirations.

Skeptical and estranged, many of our young people today look out on a world they never made. They survey its conflicts with apprehension. Graduated into the impersonal routine of a bureaucratic, technological society, many of them see life as lonely conformity lacking the lift of a driving dream.

Yet there is no greater idealism, no higher adventure than taking a realistic road for peace. It is an adventure realized not in the exhilaration of a single moment, but in the lasting rewards of patient, detailed and specific efforts —a step at a time.

—Peace requires confidence—it needs the cement of trust among friends.

—Peace requires partnership—or else we will exhaust our resources, both physical and moral, in a futile effort to dominate our friends and forever isolate our enemies.

—Peace must be just. It must answer man's dream of human dignity.

—Peace requires strength. It cannot be based on good will alone.

—Peace must be generous. No issue can be truly settled unless the solution brings mutual advantage.

—Peace must be shared. Other nations must feel that it is *their* peace just as we must feel that it is *ours*.

—And peace must be practical. It can only be found when nations resolve real issues, and accommodate each other's real interests. This requires not high rhetoric, but hard work.

These principles apply to our opponents as well as to our allies, to the less developed as well as the economically advanced nations. The peace we seek must be the work of all nations.

For peace will endure only when every nation has a greater stake in preserving than in breaking it.

I expressed these thoughts in my toast to the Acting President of India at New Delhi on July 31, 1969. I repeat it now.

"The concept of peace is as old as civilization, but the requirements of peace change with a changing world. Today we need a new definition of peace, one which recognizes not only the many threats of peace but also the many dimensions of peace.

"Peace is much more than the absence of war; and as Gandhi's life reminds us, peace is not the absence of change. Gandhi was a disciple of peace. He also was an architect of profound and far-reaching change. He stood for the achievement of change through peaceful methods, for belief in the power of conscience, for faith in the dignity and grace of the human spirit and in the rights of man.

"In today's rapidly changing world there is no such thing as a static peace or a stagnant order. To stand still is to build pressures that are bound to explode the peace; and more fundamentally, to stand still is to deny the universal aspirations of mankind. Peace today must be a creative force, a dynamic process, that embraces both the satisfaction of man's material needs and the fulfillment of his spiritual needs.

"The pursuit of peace means building a structure of stability within which the rights of each nation are respected: the rights of national independence, of self-determination, the right to be secure within its own borders and to be free from intimidation.

"This structure of stability can take many forms. Some may choose to join in formal alliances; some may choose to go their own independent way. We respect India's policy of non-alignment and its determination to play its role in the search of peace in its own way. What matters is not how peace is preserved, but that it be preserved; not the formal structure of treaties, but the informal network of common ideals and common purposes that together become a fabric of peace. What matters is not whether the principles of international behavior these represent are written or unwritten principles, but rather that they are accepted principles.

"Peace demands restraint. The truest peace expresses itself in self-restraint, in the voluntary acceptance, whether by men or by nations, of those basic rules of behavior that are rooted in mutual respect and demonstrated in mutual forbearance.

"When one nation claims the right to dictate the internal affairs of another, there is no peace.

"When nations arm for the purpose of threatening their weaker neighbors, there is no peace.

"There is true peace only when the weak are safe as the strong, only when the poor can share the benefits of progress with the rich, and only when those who cherish freedom can exercise freedom.

"Gandhi touched something deep in the spirit of man. He forced the world to confront its conscience, and the world is better for having done so. Yet we still hear other cries, other appeals to our collective conscience as a community of man.

"The process of peace is one of answering those cries, yet doing so in a manner that preserves the right of each people to seek its own destiny in its own way and strengthens the principles of national sovereignty and national integrity, on which the structure of peace among nations depends.

"However fervently we believe in our own ideals, we cannot impose those ideals on others and still call ourselves men of peace. But we can assist others who share those ideals and who seek to give them life. As fellow members of the world community, we can assist the people of India in their heroic struggle to make the world's most populous democracy a model of orderly development and progress.

"There is a relationship between peace and freedom. Because man yearns for peace, when the people are free to choose their choice is more likely to be peace among nations; and because man yearns for freedom, when peace is secure the thrust of social evolution is toward greater freedom within nations.

"Essentially, peace is rooted in a sense of community: in a recognition of the common destiny of mankind, in a respect for the common dignity of mankind, and in the patterns of cooperation that make common enterprises possible. This is why the new patterns of regional cooperation emerging in Asia can be bulwarks of peace.

"In the final analysis, however, peace is a spiritual

condition. All religions pray for it. Man must build it by reason and patience.

"On the moon, now, is a plaque bearing these simple words: 'We came in peace for all mankind.'

"Mahatma Gandhi came in peace to all mankind.

"In this spirit, then, let us all together commit ourselves to a new concept of peace:

—A concept that combines continuity and change, stability and progress, tradition and innovation;
—A peace that turns the wonders of science to the service of man;
—A peace that is both a condition and a process, a state of being and a pattern of change, a renunciation of war and a constructive alternative to revolution;
—A peace that values diversity and respects the right of different peoples to live by different systems—and freely to choose the systems they live by;
—A peace that rests on the determination of those who value it to preserve it but that looks forward to the reduction of arms and the ascendancy of reason;
—A peace responsive to the human spirit, respectful of the divinely inspired dignity of man, one that lifts the eyes of all to what man in brotherhood can accomplish and that now, as man crosses the threshold of the heavens, is more necessary than ever."